6/00

W9-AVJ-144

Knock Your Socks Off
ANSWERS

Knock Your Socks Off

ANSWERS

SOLVING CUSTOMER NIGHTMARES & SOOTHING NIGHTMARE CUSTOMERS

Kristin Anderson & Ron Zemke

amacom
American Management Association

New York • Atlanta • Boston • Chicago • Kansas City • San Francisco • Washington, D.C.
Brussels • Mexico City • Tokyo • Toronto

This publication is designed to provide accurate and authoritative
information in regard to the subject matter covered. It is sold with
the understanding that the publisher is not engaged in rendering
legal, accounting, or other professional service. If legal advice or
other expert assistance is required, the services of a competent
professional person should be sought.

Library of Congress Cataloging-in-Publication Data

Anderson, Kristin.
    Knock your socks off answers : solving customer nightmares &
  soothing nightmare customers / Kristin Anderson & Ron Zemke.
      p. cm.
    Includes bibliographical references.
    ISBN 0-8144-7884-0
    1. Customer services. 2. Consumer complaints. I. Zemke, Ron.
  II. Title.
  HF5415.5.A533   1995
  658.8'12—dc20   95-30884
                                              CIP

Printing number

10 9 8 7 6 5 4 3

Contents

Acknowledgments

Here's a sure fire way to test the patience of your friends, colleagues, coworkers, collaborators, and confidants: Tell them that you've decided to add a fourth book to a series designed to be a trilogy. Here they've all been patient, supportive, understanding and kind to a fault for four, long years—and just when they think they can stop walking on egg shells around you, and look forward to a conversation with you that isn't related to one of your darn books—you casually announce, "We've decided to do just one more Knock Your Socks Off book." We quickly learned that the best policy was to alter that message and announce instead, "Our editor has demanded that we write just one more Knock Your Socks Off book." And we are sticking to that story. Mary Glenn made us do this and so for her persistence, as well as her willingness to step up and take the blame shoulder to shoulder with us—we thank her.

We'd also like to thank our partners in crime here at Performance Research Associates for their support, sustenance, and the good ideas they contributed to this book. The guilty parties in that lineup include, but are not limited to: Jill Applegate, Chip Bell, Tom Connellan, and Karen Revill. Indictable parties at AMACOM books, in addition to Mary Glenn, include but are not limited to Weldon Rackley, Steve Arkin, Irene Majuk, Therese Mausser, Allison Loeb, Karen Wolf, and Richard Gatjens.

Three more gangs are also guilty of encouraging and egging us on and giving us good ideas: the gang at Lakewood Publications, *Lakewood Report Newsletter* (nee *The Service Edge*), the gang at Padgett-Thompson, and the gang at Kaset International. Last but not least, a very, very special thanks to the Salvador Dali of our effort—John Bush.

Kristin Anderson Ron Zemke
Minneapolis, MN Minneapolis, MN

Introduction:
About This Book

Jim was steamed—frustrated, really—and it showed. An hour into our seminar on delivering high-quality customer service, he was on his feet eloquently denouncing our "Do what it takes to make the customer right" philosophy and defending his own view that "Customers are no-good dirty rotten finks," at least some of them. At least some of the time. At least the one who had fired him when her lawn died last summer. After she overwatered it. After Jim had explicitly warned her of the consequences. After she promised she wouldn't change the settings on the automatic watering system.

Jim is a landscape professional. In his words:

> I've studied hard to be able to do my job. I went to school for it. But customers don't treat me like a professional. They think anyone with a shovel and a lawnmower can be a landscaper. And if you work outside, you can't be smart. I know what I'm doing and what I'm talking about, but they don't want to hear that. They never listen to me.

It's not hard to understand Jim's frustration—and his hope that our seminar would provide him with a few magic words and clever phrases that would convince future clients to listen up, toe the mark, not talk back, and in general solve his perceived Rodney Dangerfield problem. We would have loved to have been able to turn to Jim at that moment with big toothy grins and an announcement by one of us that would have gone something like this:

> Jim, I'm really glad you brought that up. Yes, ladies and gentlemen, I hold right here in my hand a simple 3"-by-4" plastic-coated card. It's slightly larger than an

ace of spades and can be carried easily in pocket or purse. Step up a little closer. On careful inspection you will note that printed right here on the obverse and reverse sides of this one small, easy-to-read,-store and -carry card are seventeen scintillating phrases, the product of over 60,000 interviews with top-notch customer service professionals in 200 of the world's best organizations, that are unconditionally guaranteed to double your ability to definitively answer the ten stupidest questions and seven toughest objections proffered by customers of certified customer service professionals like yourselves.

Didn't happen. Can't.

What Jim is wishing for, the awe of expertise, the "Yes, Doctor, no, Doctor, thank you very much, Doctor" respect for professional competence, doesn't exist today. Not even Marcus Welby could command it. Today's average customer is too educated, knowledgeable, time-driven, value-oriented, opinionated, skeptical, and exposed to too many "professionals" to be reverential in the way Jim would like his customers to be. In the face of this new, more demanding customer, attainment of Jim's desire for respect as a professional hinges on a lot more than a degree, certification, a clean white shirt, and a business card. In addition to professional competence, Jim needs poise and patience.

The word *poise*, in *Webster's New Collegiate Dictionary*, has two distinct and applicable meanings. The first has to do with balance: "to hold [something] supported or suspended without motion in a steady position." The second concerns personal bearing and manner: Exhibiting an "easy, self-possessed, assurance of manner; [showing] gracious tact in coping or handling"; in other words, having interactions with others unmarred by rancor, conflict or angry outbursts.

To show poise in service delivery is, first, to suspend insistence on one's own expertise in favor of balancing the needs and wants of the customer with one's own sense and understanding of what's right, acceptable, and doable. Equally important is conducting that negotiation in an atmosphere of equanimity and with a feeling of partnership. The service deliverer needs to find ways to give the customer the sense of security that comes from working with a knowledgeable professional, without undermining or threatening the customer's decisional prerogatives and leaving intact the customer's sense of control over the situation.

Tactically, that means things like looking for the areas of easy agreement with the customer before taking on the issue or issues that seem to be in contention:

> "Yes, Mrs. Haversham, I certainly agree that your lawn isn't as full and rich-looking as some in your neighborhood."

It can also mean looking for ways to educate subtly, rather than telling and directing:

> "Sometimes, Mrs. Haversham, there is a trade-off between a thick, lush lawn and quiet shade. You have quite a few large mature trees on your property. You might want to decide which is the best overall look for various parts of your lawn."

It might also mean creatively compromising with the customer's desires:

> "Mrs. Haversham, I'm apprehensive about so much watering. If this schedule is overambitious, your grass could be damaged before we have a chance to talk about changing it. I can, however, get a ground saturation meter and show you how to use it so that you can monitor exactly what is going on and so that you can observe water conditions more closely than usual."

In the last analysis, there are often several conflicting forces at play in a service situation. These include:

- The wants and expectations of the customer
- The knowledge and skill of the service provider—and

the provider's desire to use them in the best way for the customer
- The mutual understanding that, in the last analysis, the economic yea and nay are always and forever the customer's

The true professional never loses sight of the importance of any, and the need to balance all, of these forces.

Wait a second, you two!

Just what the dickens is this book about if not specific answers to difficult questions; like it suggests on the cover?

Glad you asked that question, Jim. (You'll just have to imagine the toothy grin.)

Yes, this book, as advertised, does contain some very good, very specific answers to some very nasty—as in hard-to-handle—customer questions, comments, and situations. Our suggested answers aren't something we baked up in the back office one day last January during a snowstorm. They are answers we have accumulated from four years of "Knock Your Socks Off Service"® seminars conducted by us and by others, from hours of dialogue with other experts in the customer service biz, from our focus group research into customer "druthers," and from two lifetimes of customer service work. Most important, these answers come from hundreds of your peers who have tried them out and told us that they do indeed work back on the job, day after day, one customer at a time.

Just the same, we don't believe in magic words or silver bullet phrases, save perhaps "Please" and "Thank you very much." We believe that the best answers to tough customer questions come from understanding the reasons behind those tough questions and from having a good working theory of what you want to accomplish with the customer, once you have drawn a bead on the wants, needs, attitudes, fears, and hopes behind the tough question, sharp comment, or antagonistic retort.

Bearing all that in mind, here are some things you need to know to make the best use of this book.

First, "Knock Your Socks Off Answers" is divided into six sections.

Part 1:   Pat Answers to Peevish Questions and Provocative Customer Comments

This first part of the book deals with thirty very common, tough-to-deal-with questions, comments, and challenges and with some great answers we've heard and used and that we stand behind. What makes the majority of these questions tough isn't their technical content. Some are meant to be provocative or argumentative. Others challenge your ability to be tactful. All are easy questions to stub your toe on. They are the sorts of questions, comments, and verbal jabs that just beg for a witty answer or cutting reply but that lead to no end of trouble if you give into the temptation.

Part 2:   Smart Answers to Even Tougher Questions

Here we look at tough questions of a different variety. These are customer questions, comments, and complaints that are "meaty." They are based in the customer's sense of what is right or in what the customer thinks ought to be done. Accordingly, the answers depend more on getting your point of view across to the customer than on the "stylishness" or cleverness of your answer. Tact is involved, but so is content. The principles or ideas behind the answers are as important as the actual answers we suggest.

Part 3:   Questions With No Easy Answers

Some customer questions have no easy answers. These are the "It's only one day out of warranty! What do you mean you won't replace it?" kinds of questions. Questions that make us squirm and twist when we hear them because they strike an empathetic chord in us. Questions the answers to which will just not make the customer a happy camper—period. There are, as the section title indicates, no easy answers to these questions, but we will share with you what we've learned.

Part 4:   Getting Service as Good as You Give

As we have watched and listened to great service providers "doing their thing," we've been struck by how much easier some customers are to do business with and how readily service people go above and beyond for some customers. It isn't about age, race, sex, color, creed, politics, or a shared fanaticism for the same sports teams. It's about time and attention. We've also noticed that great service providers tend to be great service receivers. In Part 4 then, we discuss what we've learned about receiving as well as giving great service.

Part 5:   Customers Say the Darnedest Things

This is a section we couldn't resist writing. It's all those things that fall into the category of "I can't believe he said that," those things our world-class customer service experts swear to us on a stack of religious tomes that customers have said, asked for, and blurted out with—for the most part—the straightest of faces. They made us laugh, shake our heads, sigh, and just plain giggle—so we couldn't resist sharing them with you. Think of Part 5 as one part tonic, one part reward for your hard work, and three parts stress relief medication.

Appendix: Recommended Resources

In the appendix, we offer our list of the best customer service resources—books, video- and audiotape programs, newsletters, and the like—for continually improving your customer service skills.

Finally, we want you to know that we believe that this book is a starting point for your advanced professional development—not an end-all, be-all cookbook designed to solve your every customer service problem. That would be an oversell and dishonest and not in the true spirit of service. We strongly suggest that, as you and your customer service colleagues read this book and think about our answers, you spend some time creating your own even better answers or, at the very least, deciding which of the answers we suggest are the best answers for your company, your department, and your customers.

And now for the disclaimer.

Just as we are confident that you will find these Knock Your Socks Off Answers helpful and useful in your customer service situations, it is equally true that not one of them will be absolutely perfect for your situation. To make them work best for you, you will need to mold and modify them for use in your organization and department. We believe that this will work best if you and a team of your colleagues come together, look at our questions and answers, decide how the tough questions you deal with are different, and together create a "better yet" set of answers, ones that will work best for your unique, specific situations.

Now, with all that out of the way, let's have at it, and welcome to *Knock Your Socks Off Answers: Solving Customer Nightmares and Soothing Nightmare Customers*.

Part 1

Pat Answers to Peevish Questions and Provocative Customer Comments

A soft answer turneth away wrath.

Proverbs 15:1

The customer who's always right probably waits on himself.

Laurence J. Peter
Author, *The Peter Principle*

A great comeback makes your day.

Anonymous

It's a good answer that knows when to stop.

Italian proverb

Who among us hasn't been in the shower the day after a customer has unjustly and uncivilly climbed all over us and imagined a rematch, wherein we fix that awful person with a steely eye and, in a voice crisp as a January morning in Maine, render the rascal speechless? And contrite. And begging our forgiveness. A great, ego-satisfying daydream.

Back on the job, we all know that killer comebacks have one unfortunate side effect: More often than not, they send the customer packing—for good.

That said, there are any number of situations that the customer service professional faces in which a preplanned, prepracticed, well-thought-out response will soothe the irate customer, smooth the troubled waters, avert misunderstandings, save face, and allow you to move the service transaction toward a positive completion and not leave you feeling like a tread-upon doormat.

What follows are pat answers to thirty peevish questions and provocative customer comments that are both commonly voiced and difficult to deal with. They are presented one at a time, dissected for their real meaning, and answered.

"Why are you changing? I liked the old way!"

The one constant about companies today is that they are constantly changing their policies, procedures, methods, operations, and the way they deal with the customer. We face it every day. Customers are no happier about new procedures than you probably are. The amount of change in our lives—and in the lives of the people we serve—can feel overwhelming.

Companies make changes for a lot of reasons: The old way cost too much, new technology is now available (or finally made it into the budget), customer needs have changed, and, of course, the time-honored "just because." Much of the resistance customers—and all of us—have to change comes from the feeling that change is being done *to* us, rather than *for* us. It's no wonder confused and concerned customers cry out:

"Why are you changing? I liked the old way!"

One approach to calming customers' concerns is to let customers see themselves as participants in the change. There are two ways to do that. The first reinforces customer involvement in the original decision, even though the individual customer you are speaking with may not have been personally involved. As long as a representative sample of customers was contacted, try saying:

"Changing was a difficult decision for us. We did an extensive customer study. You may even have received a phone call or survey. We based this redesign on what we learned. I think you'll be surprised to see how much easier this is."

3

A second option is to ask customers to evaluate the changes you've made in processes, procedures, or forms. This answer is particularly useful immediately following the change:

> *"When you've had a chance to look at the new account summary form, would you complete a comment card or give me a call with your reactions to it? I really value your opinion."*

One caution: Don't seek feedback you never plan to use. This pat answer becomes an empty answer—and a waste of time for you and your customer—if the customer comments are never read and considered.

Variation 1: "You people have really gotten chintzy, haven't you?"

Sometimes customers seem to have a mental scorecard for evaluating your company's changes. They want to hear the underlying motivation for the change in order to mark it as fair or foul. They are not so much concerned with *what* you've changed, but *why*. If dollars and cents (or francs or pesos or marks or yen) are at the root of the change, *mention the money*. Everyone understands rising costs. If you were losing money the old way, it's okay to say so. If the customer understands why the procedure or process needed to be changed but still finds the change to be a problem, invite her to (a) try it and (b) give you any suggestions for an alternative change. Consider:

> **"Hey, these used to come packed in individual boxes! What's going on here? Are you getting cheap?"**

> *"We just can't afford to deliver Crunchie Wunchies in the old way at the old price. So, we've made some packaging changes that allow us to keep the same low price."*

You may combine this answer with the involve-the-customer tactic we discussed earlier.

> *"We had to either raise our prices or change the way we did business. We asked our customer advisory panel and they said 'protect us from the price increase,' so we made a packaging change."*

Variation 2: "You're worried about a lawsuit, aren't you?"

When a change is implemented to protect you and your company from liability—monetary or other—you need to explain the change with a very carefully planned statement. Don't get caught in a discussion of the details. For example, a child day-care center employee would never want to say, *"We used to give children a ride home if their parents couldn't pick them up at the day-care center, but after that four-car accident Cindy had—she's the one with the long dark hair—well, our insurance says we can't drive the kids around anymore. Can you believe it?"* Saying the wrong thing can raise more ire and concern than saying nothing. So think it through first and then have your answer ready to play out as soon as your customer asks the question. Consider:

> *"Your child is as precious to us as she is to you. We'll keep your child safe within the day-care center property from the time you release her to our care in the morning to the time you or an adult you designate in advance picks her up in the afternoon. Because our personal vehicles are not day-care center property, we are not able to drive the children in them."*

You don't have to tell a customer everything about everything you know. It's even possible to overtell your customer, to give more information than the customer cares to know. Your answers should give customers a little insight, enough to satisfy their curiosity, thank them for their interest and concern, and then get you both back to the real business at hand.

"What do you mean your price went up?"

It is hard to avoid price hikes for any length of time, especially without a corresponding reduction in the size or quantity of product purchased. Just ask your grandmother or grandfather how big a chocolate bar was when she or he was a child. Here are four tips for responding to price hike questions:

First, *allow the customer to tell you about his or her frustration,* and sometimes even anger, about the price hikes. Get that frustration out of the way so that you both can move on.

"I can understand how frustrating it is when prices increase. That's why we've worked so hard to avoid it."

Second, *offer concrete justification* for the price hike. For example:

"Paper costs have skyrocketed in the past year, and we've finally been forced to pass on some of that cost."

Third, *build a connection* by comparing your cost increase to other cost increases you and the customer may both be experiencing in your private lives. Remind the customer that your company isn't the only company raising prices:

"I know that I've been seeing a price increase at the grocery store for paper products such as paper towels, napkins, and the like."

Finally, *if only one element of your cost of doing business is increasing*—for example, shipping and handling fees—*you should point out that anomaly* to your customer.

"Actually, the cost per item is the same. The increase in price comes from the increasing fees we are charged to deliver products directly to your door."

Variation 1: "Why can't you cut me a deal?"

In some cultures, and especially for some products, a listed price is only a starting point. The final price will be negotiated between each buyer and the seller. If you are part of a Detroit, Michigan, car dealership or a Cancun craft market, you are probably used to customers who are seeking a "real deal." Difficulty arises, however, when you lack the latitude or authority to dicker with customers over price.

Your best bet: Whether it is your call or someone else's, *know exactly when and how much of a discount or deal is available to customers.* This means keeping in touch with advertising and promotion specials, with the price breaks for preferred customers, and with what the competition is charging for the same goods. Think of customers' desire for a "deal" as an opportunity, not a threat. When customers ask for a volume discount, for example, you may be able to use that request to increase the size of the sale. We heard a telephone sales representative for a pet care product manufacturer explain:

> **"I can give you a 20 percent discount if you order an entire pallet of dog food, just two bags more than you normally purchase."**

Variation 2: "They're selling the same thing for less money just down the street."

If you're a retailer, the last thing you want to hear on a busy Saturday morning is:

> **"Why, I just saw this down the street—and it was on sale for 20 percent less than your price."**

You know all about promotional specials and loss leaders, and you know that most of time those discounts don't last very long. And you know as well that the competitor who is running the special probably received a price break from the supplier, just for this one special-price sale. And you know that your customer could not care less.

Your best bet: *Express surprise and explain.*

> **"Oh, really? I wish we could meet that price. Quite likely, their sale price is based on a special price they were given by the manufacturer."**

It may be that the other store is selling a product that *looks* the same as yours but that is not actually identical. *Point out the differences*. This may also be a good time to remind your customer of the quality service you sell with every product.

> *"The computer they are advertising is the same brand. However, it is the Advantage model, built for home use. The Bravo model, sold only through dealers, was built for the office with components that can stand up to rougher, industrial treatment. In addition, when you buy from us you have our service team to answer questions and provide assistance."*

Variation 3: "That comes with free delivery, doesn't it?"

Sometimes a customer will want to change the terms of the sale after the sale is made. Often this pops up on large-ticket items just before the customer hands over the cash:

> **"Oh, delivery is included when I buy a sofa, isn't it? I only live a few states away."**

In these cases you must know ahead of time what you will and won't, what you can and can't do and what you are able to throw in to sweeten the deal. Resist the temptation to become resentful of customers' last-minute requests for "extras."

> *"I'm sorry, but we offer free delivery only within the metropolitan area. I can offer you this fine antimacassar—it will look great on your couch when you get it home."*

A word of caution: Extras and exceptions may set a precedent you aren't ready or willing to live up to. We preach, "Treat customers the way they want to be treated." But there are times when, for the greater good of the company and to ensure fairness for all customers, it is more important for you to be consistent.

There is a place for bending the rules and breaking land speed records for customers. However, there are times to say no or, better yet, to say no by offering an alternative. For example, our sofa buyer may be satisfied to know that delivery is available, for a price:

> *"Our delivery area doesn't extend that far, but I can coordinate a delivery driver for you if you'd like. The fee would be $75. Shall I do that for you now?"*

"Why are you looking it up? Don't you just know?"

Customers not only expect customer service people to have access to vast amounts of knowledge when they ask for that information; they expect them to provide it immediately and off the top of their heads. "I've got a quick and easy question for you" are words to strike fear in every service provider's heart. If your job is troubleshooting or repair, you understand this very well. As Stan Davis and Jim Botkin wrote in the September/October 1994 *Harvard Business Review*, "As recently as 1965, a mechanic who had absorbed 500 pages of repair manuals could fix just about any car on the road. Today that same mechanic would need to have read nearly 500,000 pages of manuals, equivalent to some 300 Manhattan telephone books." Yet, every day, thousands of customers ask service providers this question:

While I enter Your complaint into our computer, Perhaps You'd like To look through an album of our service awards.

"Why are you looking it up? Don't you just know?"

Customer expectations about your technical knowledge may or may not be fair. After all, would you be comfortable with a surgeon who had to take the manual into her most basic operations? But fair isn't the issue. The issue is fear—fear the problem won't be fixed or won't be fixed right the first time. Your answer must *put the fear to rest* and bolster the customer's confidence in you. Service technicians offer a variety of responses that work. The simplest is:

"You know the old rule—measure twice, cut once. I want to make sure I've got everything right."

Sometimes that isn't quite enough. The customer wants to know why you need to check a book to "make sure." In that case, briefly explain:

"This machine comes in five different models. I'm just doublechecking the protocol for this model."

At other times, the "don't you know" question can provide an opening for customer education. Help the customer understand and feel comfortable using the manuals:

"The exact calibrations for this machine depend on the material you are using with it. I'm resetting them according to our chart. Let me show you."

When the customer fears a negative outcome—that what's broken will stay broken or that in-route shipments will never arrive—they want to know that their service provider is in control. Showing you do know and you are trained is as much about attitude as about the words you say. Calm fear by demonstrating confidence in yourself, your training, and your organization's support network.

"Why should
I believe you?"

Customers call or walk into your place of business, ask for information, present problems, and request help. Most of the time, they ask, you tell, they are satisfied, and life goes on. Most of the time. From time to time, however, a customer will respond to your wise counsel or sage advice with a curt and unfriendly "Why should I believe anything *you* say?" When that happens it's unnerving and occasionally even insulting, especially when you know that what you are saying *is* the truth and *is* what the customer needs to know or hear or do *and* that a good many customers have profited from taking your advice in the past. Sometimes the phrasing is a little less confrontational. But the questions and comments—"Are you sure about that?" and "That doesn't seem right to me" and "That can't be true"—are, at their core, the same simple, untrusting question:

"Why should I believe you?"

It may be that the customer is simply doubting your organization's ability to do what you are promising or proposing. In selling, they call it a "no-trust" problem. The customer simply doesn't think your organization can or will do what you say it will. Your best recourse is to *share evidence of your past performance*. Share your track record, your surveys and testimonials, and so on. Be ready with references and time lines. If you are dealing face to face, you might write down your promise and give a copy to the customer.

Take steps to prove your *reliability*, your ability to deliver on your promises. Take the evidence in hand, step forward, and say:

"That's a really good question. You don't have to take my word for it. We have hundreds of satisfied

customers. Let me show you exactly how we can create the same results for you."

Or you may go directly to your proof:

"That's a great question. We have a long history of satisfied customers. I'd be pleased to put you in contact with several of them so that they can tell you personally about the quality of our work. Now, may I show you exactly what I think we can do for you?"

Variation 1: "You people never do what you promise!"

Sometimes this blunt, lack-of-trust trial statement may come up because you are in an industry that has a history of customer upset or a well-publicized bad mark on its record. The strategy, then, is to *distance yourself and the solution you are offering* from the industry or from the negative event the customer has in the back of his or her mind. Consider this real-life example:

"You're a cable TV company. Why should I believe that your installer will even bother to show up?"

"Here at Continental Cablevision of St. Paul, we've earned a national reputation for great service. Why, we even won kudos from TV Guide!"

Okay, your company may not have been in *TV Guide*, but it probably wasn't featured on "60 Minutes" last night, either. Your company has a record to lean on and colors to fly. Don't be timid—fly them.

Variation 2: "You'll just mess it up again."

A variation on "I don't trust you" arises when something has *indeed* gone wrong in the past and trust must be rebuilt. It may have been a company or personal error—a computer error that wiped out a customer order or a message you forgot to give to the accounts receivable department. Or it may be that the problem was caused by an act of nature but you have been given the blame—"Don't you people have plans to deal with snow?" When the once-bitten, twice-doubting customer confronts you with a stern and challenging:

"What makes this time any different from last time, when you ruined my life?"

Be prepared to dig in, own up, and guarantee that this time will be different:

"You're right. Our company promises forty-eight-hour turnaround, and it didn't happen last time. Today, I am personally going to take care of your order. Here's exactly what I'm going to do."

Variation 3: "You just don't want to."

Sometimes, even after you've outlined what you can and cannot do for a particular customer, the "I don't trust you" attitude resurfaces. The customer may not be willing to let go of his or her skepticism and mistrust. The customer counters that you are simply trying to get out of doing what you really ought to do, which, of course, is whatever the customer demands. It is critical at this point to *keep your cool*. Avoid "Yes, it is/No, it isn't" arguments with your customer—they are impossible to win. And your customer probably isn't ready to hear and accept the facts of the case the way you see them anyway. Your goal is not to change this angry challenger into a supporter. It is to be so consistent, so respectful, and so sincerely concerned about doing whatever is possible to assist the customer that later he or she will realize you spoke the truth—and next time you will be believed.

"That can't be true. You have to be able to track that package—you just don't want to spend the time to do it!"

"I really wish I could track it. Unfortunately, the contract carrier you specified doesn't offer real-time tracking. What I can tell you is the package left our warehouse on Friday afternoon by truck. I will get an update from the shipper in the morning and will be able to call you then. Again, I am very sorry you are experiencing this frustration."

"What could you possibly know about this?"

Customers today are looking for information and knowledge, and, according to a survey by the *Washington Post*, they are having a hard time finding it. According to the *Post*, the number one irritation for department store shoppers is service representatives who know less about the merchandise than do customers. And retail isn't the only area where customers believe expertise is commonly absent. Experiences with all sorts of businesses have convinced some customers that they are the smart ones—and service providers . . . well, what could we possibly know? Some customers question and doubt almost everything they are told—be it about product quality or delivery schedules. Sometimes it's subtle. Customers may gather information from a variety of service providers and then take it home to compare with a resource such as *Consumer Reports* or another "real" expert. Or they may demand to talk to a supervisor or manager or "someone who knows something." Whether they express it through words or actions, the message is the same:

"What could you possibly know about this?"

It's frustrating when the customer won't allow you to help. After all, you've been trained for just that task. And a constant undercurrent of "I'll just wait and see if that's true" will put anyone on the defensive. In these situations *ask for a chance* to be of service. Challenge your customer head-on to allow you to help and to give you a chance to prove your knowledge and worth. It's almost unheard of not to give someone a chance when she asks for it. Simply say:

"Please give me a chance to assist you."

It sounds so simple, but it is so effective. There are, however, situations where it is not quite enough—times when the customer has a specific reason, valid or invalid, for believing you don't know anything. In those cases, you need to address the customer's specific concern.

Variation 1: "You don't have a track record."

It may be that your organization is new to the business, new to the area, or new to the customer. With the paint still wet on the door and your business cards on order, you'll need to *create a sense of history*—a past that anchors your company and gives a firm sense of credibility. Consider:

"The ink is still wet on your stationery. What could you people know about this business?"

"Our company offers a fresh perspective, backed by the many years of industry experience of our principals. All told, we have over forty-five years of experience solving problems and serving customers in this industry. Please give us a chance to assist you."

Sometimes that sense of history can come from an association or affiliation with a larger, more well-known organization. If you work in a branch office or as part of a franchise, point to the strength of the parent organization. For example:

"When we opened our doors for business as a new franchisee, we brought the entire weight of the XYZ franchise organization with us. Please give us a chance to assist you."

Variation 2: "What could a *woman* know about trucks?"

Sometimes it's not the organization that is in question, but you personally. Perhaps you aren't the size, race, height, gender, creed, or type of person your customer expected to see. Or you might seem to be too young or too old, too hip or too conservative, to have the right knowledge, experience, or perspective. It's frustrating. You are qualified for the job, even if you aren't what the customer expected to see. To get a chance to prove you are indeed qualified, keep the conversation friendly and nondefensive, but don't be shy about letting your customer know what you can do. In short, *you've got to flaunt it . . .* with a smile.

"Well, little lady, what could you possibly know about driving a tractor trailer?"

"Well, I've never driven long-haul for a living, but I sure have changed the tires, checked the oil, and spent a lot of hours on the test track learning about trucks like yours. Why don't you tell me what parts you need to order and see if I can't help you?"

For the woman we know who created this response, it wasn't bragging—she could do it. She had all the training and experience you could possibly imagine. Don't overstate your credentials; just emphasize your training and your background if you are challenged on your expertise. And do it in a nice way. Perhaps you haven't driven forty hours on a test track or assembled an engine, but you've got the job and you've been trained for it. Make sure your customer knows you are competent and confident. Consider this exchange at a home hardware center between a customer and a rather young sales associate:

Sales Associate: I think I can recommend just the right paint for your basement walls.

Customer: Maybe I'd better wait and talk with someone else.

Sales Associate: You're certainly welcome to do that. Our top-rated sealers are located right over here. Let me point out the one I'd recommend so that you can consider it while you wait. It's this one—a new offering from our most popular paint company. Several customers have already used it with great results.

Customer: Hum. Let me take a look at that. Great results, you say?

The sales associate was able to win this customer's trust by demonstrating knowledge and confidence.

Variation 3: "Don't tell me that you understand!"

Perhaps the hardest variation on "What could you possibly know" to deal with is the one rooted in some truth. For instance, you have offered a well-intended "Gee, I really understand your situation," and the customer explodes with "You couldn't possibly understand" or becomes sarcastic: "Oh, *really?*"

Back off, and redirect the customer to the business at hand. Consider this example from a children's photo studio:

Customer: You don't have kids. How could you possibly understand what it's like to keep four kids clean for forty minutes while we wait to have their pictures taken?

Associate: You're right, I don't. And thank goodness you're here to help me. Tell me what I need to do to make this work for you.

Enlisting the customer to help you make use of your expertise, the skill and knowledge she came to you for in the first place, often breaks the barrier. You are, in essence, saying:

"No, I don't know more than you do about your business and situation. I am an expert in my job. Between us, we should be able to make this work."

"What do you mean you can't tell me my son's grades? I paid for them."

Solving customer nightmares and soothing nightmare customers often rests on your tact and sensitivity, your ability to practice diplomacy. Here are four diplomacy issues that seem to come up frequently for service professionals.

"What do you mean you *can't* tell me my own son's grades? I pay the tuition, you know."

Right-to-privacy laws limit the information you and your organization can share about your customers—including students over the age of eighteen. Sometimes, the legal right to privacy conflicts with other *perceived* rights—such as the right of a parent to know his or her own college kid's grades or the right of an adult child to oversee the finances of an aging parent. In such cases, without a signed release, those perceived rights cannot be granted. Your response, which you may have to repeat more than once for it to be heard:

> *"I am sorry. Your son is certainly lucky to have you for a parent. As you might expect, we are bound by the privacy act and can release information about grades only with a written authorization from the student."*

Variation 1: "Where's Nancy? I always work with Nancy."

Whenever an employee leaves your organization—be it to take a better job, because of a layoff, or because she has been "made available to the marketplace"—you can count on hearing the "Where's Nancy?" question from customers and coworkers. Without express, written permission from Nancy, there really isn't much you can or should say—especially if you know Nancy was involuntarily released.

> *"Nancy has left the firm to pursue other opportunities. Your account is now being handled by Pat. May I transfer you?"*

If a customer insists on contacting Nancy, resist any impulse to share home address and phone number. Instead:

> *"I'm sorry. We aren't allowed to give out home address information. However, if you'd like to send Nancy a note via our firm, I would be happy to see that it is forwarded to her home."*

Variation 2: "How's business?"

It seems like such an innocuous question: "How's business?" Customers often know us well and share, rightly or wrongly, details about their own organizations. So it seems natural to answer questions about our own organization. However, that type of question-and-answer session often invites us to share details and information that are really not the business of our customers. For that reason, we are fond of the response we once heard from Jim Miller, author of *Corporate Coach* (St. Martin's Press, 1993):

> *"Business is terrific!"*

When asked to elaborate, Jim continues:

> *"I have a job, I get a paycheck, and I get to work with great customers like you. It really is terrific."*

It is especially important to have an answer ready when your company has been in the headlines, for whatever reason. Your response will have to change to fit the situation. Consider this from a "survivor" whose organization had just gone through well-publicized layoffs:

> *"I think the economy is affecting every business. Tighter times force us to reevaluate how we do business. It's hard, but in the end it will help us compete."*

Variation 3: "How can you live with yourself, selling cigarettes and dirty magazines in this grocery store!"

When customers come to us with a prejudgment or complaint about us personally or about the organization for which we work, it's important not to become defensive. The grocery store in which we heard the above question has a simple response:

> *"I'm sorry you find those things offensive. If you would like, here is a comment card for you to fill out. That way we'll be able to better respond to your concerns. The card goes straight to the owner. Thank you!"*

As the owner explained, "At first I thought I'd just ignore the complaints—after all, those products are selling. That's why I stock them. But as I've listened, I've learned more about my customers than I ever did before. And cigarettes and magazines? I'm now more careful about where I display them. And, well, if there comes a day when more customers object than buy, I just may stop selling them altogether."

"This has to be the ugliest dress I've ever seen!"

You don't have to travel any farther than your own TV to see that we live in an era of diversity and personal expression. That creates quite a challenge for service organizations seeking to meet the individual needs of masses of customers.

Consider the world of retail. Customers aren't shy about letting us know: "This isn't my color—I doubt it's anybody's color."

"This has to be the ugliest dress I've ever seen! What was your buyer thinking?!"

Whether the criticism is delivered in a tone of genuine puzzlement or as a scathing indictment, it's hard not to become defensive when the judgment called into question is yours—or your organization's. Your pat answer should allow you and your customer to *agree to disagree*, or at least to ignore the difference in judgment and move on. It's okay if your customer doesn't like the model or product in question—and has no idea who would. If the customer continues to criticize, make a show of recording the customer's comments, and then move on.

Responding to comments like, "This has to be the ugliest dress I've ever seen" requires wording that you, the service professional, are personally comfortable delivering. Use our wording as a model, and then substitute words that are both comfortable for you and appropriate for your situation. Whatever words you use, the tone and intent must remain pleasant and positive:

"I have to admit, it wasn't one of my favorites either, but our buyer tells us it's the latest rage in

Paris. And it does look great on some women. Let me show you some other things."

Or:

"This is one of those dresses you either love or you hate, and I think I know where you stand. Let me show you some other things."

Variation: "What a dumb calling plan."

When matching a customer with just the right product or service, customer service professionals begin assessing the customer and his or her needs almost from the moment the phone rings or the customer walks in the door. The right match is usually found, but not always. Sometimes the poor fit occurs because the customer didn't tell us everything about his or her needs; other times the service provider made a wrong assumption; still other times, there's simply a difference of opinion. Whatever the reason, you needn't be defensive. Your pat answer to a mismatch should *deflect* any anger or ire created by the mismatch and then *redirect* or deflect the customer on to another option, something more suitable to his or her tastes, needs, wants, and expectations. Consider:

"This is the stupidest long-distance calling plan I've ever heard of! Anyone who can afford to call overseas doesn't need a discount!"

"That may be. Since you do most of your long-distance calling within your state, that plan is probably not for you. We do have a plan designed just for the type of calling you do. Let me explain it to you."

Finding just the right things for your customer is always a guessing game. It's not uncommon to miss with your first try, or your second, and sometimes your third. The point is not to get derailed over your customer's reasons for not liking what you suggest. Keep moving forward.

"Don't you people keep records? I did this already!"

In today's high-speed, high-tech world, we *expect* service providers to know all about us. Call to order a pizza, and likely as not you will hear, "Would you like your usual pepperoni, pineapple, and extra-cheese pizza, extra large? Or would you like to try something new?" Check into certain hotels, and the desk clerk will greet you with "Welcome back. I see you prefer a smoking room with two beds near the elevator and the ice machine. I've got just the one." And all that before you've done much more than identify yourself.

Thanks to technology, the local grocery store can track your shopping habits and then offer you coupons targeted to your needs. The water and electric meters can read themselves over the telephone line, and back at your office the photocopy machine may call in for service via a modem connection. It's no wonder our customers expect us to know every detail of their service history—and to read their minds about what they'll need in the future.

Despite what customers may think about all this wonderful technology, you and we know most companies haven't reached the height of database integration and keystroke ease. Customer data may be captured but difficult to access.

Think about your own experience at the pharmacy counter of your local drug store. Doesn't it give you a feeling of security when your pharmacist verifies your current prescription against the prescription you were given the last time you had your medication refilled? Verifying data at the time of service may be the best way to keep database information current—in some situations it may be the only way to ensure up-to-date, accurate information. Unfortunately, it can also irritate your customer. Ask a returning hospital patient to fill out admittance forms and you may well hear:

27

"Don't you people keep records? I already did this last month! I hope you remember what you removed last time."

In those situations where verification of the information is an imperative, say so. *Give customers a reason* to give you the information again. Consider this favorite response we heard from a hospital admissions clerk:

> *"You'd be surprised how much information can change between one visit and the next. Our system is designed to ensure we have the most accurate information possible so we can continue to give you the best medical care available."*

Or, if you prefer your pat answer to be shorter and crisper:

> *"We take your medical history every time to ensure we have it correct and up-to-date."*

Variation 1: "She has my number."

A classic and related situation occurs when you take a phone message from a long-time customer or supplier. Even though the caller is well known, you want your message to be complete and accurate. You ask for the caller's name and confirm the spelling. You write down the caller's company and then ask for the telephone number and receive a curt "She has my number." You can almost hear the caller thinking, "I told you I was returning her call. That means that she must have my number or she couldn't have called me. Don't you people keep records?" There is a simple way to avoid the entire issue. When you get to the phone number, ask:

"May I have your number for quick reference, please?"

It's the "for quick reference" part that gives the caller a reason and stops his or her resistance. You acknowledge that, yes, you do have the information in some appropriate place and request the customer provide it again, anyway, just to make everyone's life a little easier.

Variation 2: "How many times do you want me to fill out this survey?"

There are also situations where you truly didn't mean to ask for the same customer information twice. In these cases your customer's "I already did this" may be your clue that there is a system problem. If so, *apologize*, and, if the problem *may* happen again, say so. Explain what the customer should realistically expect. If you don't, customers will expect that once they talk with you, everything will be fixed, and they'll never be asked twice again. Here's an example from a consumer goods company.

> **"I already got one of these customer service survey forms. How many are you going to send me? Didn't you read the first one?"**

> *"I'm sorry that happened. Thank you for letting me know we already surveyed you. Perhaps in our effort to be responsive, we were a little too enthusiastic. I appreciate your candor. If this is a problem with the survey system, you may receive another survey or two before it's corrected. If you've already filled one out, why don't you ignore those future surveys. However, if you do have any additional insights or ideas, please let us know. In the meantime, I'm going to bring this issue to the right people."*

As we perfect our information systems, we know more and more about our customers—what they like and dislike, what they buy and how they use it, and what they may need and value in the future. At the same time, our customers are becoming more and more demanding about how we access, use, and share what we know about them. Knowing why your company collects information will help ensure that you gather accurate information during your encounters with customers.

"You're nice, but those other people. . . ."

For some customers, the most important part of being served is the one-to-one relationship you create with them. Those customers with whom you establish a very personal relationship, customers who clearly see you as a friend and advocate, will often be more open and honest about their needs and expectations. They will tell you what they like and what they don't like—valuable information you can use to improve your own performance and the success of your organization. Sometimes these very personable relationships can spawn an interesting and potentially hard-to-deal-with effect—the temptation to commiserate. While would-be commiserators are sharing their own "ain't it awful" stories about work and life situations, you can simply nod and smile, or frown, when appropriate.

When customers turn the tables and want you to tell them about the "ain't it awful" parts of your job, be alert. "It's the same old story everywhere, isn't it?" they might ask. The expectation is that because they shared a little dirt with you, you in turn will give them the inside lowdown on your company, department, or colleagues. It's called "psychological reciprocity." You have no obligation to oblige, but you need to respond in a way that doesn't hurt your strong relationship with the customer. The question is, what do you say in response to:

"You're nice, but those other people! When I talk with them, I feel like I'm imposing."

If you agree that the people you work with, or that the company you work for, really doesn't care—"Ya, I know exactly what you mean!"—you will be inviting the customer to continue. That won't help you accomplish your service task. And, in the long run, it won't show you in the best light, either. After all, you've chosen to work with "those other people." Rather than agree, your response should *express concern* about the customer's experience and *affirm the customer's importance*.

> **"I'm really sorry to hear you felt that way. We wouldn't have jobs if it weren't for customers like you."**

When you personally are customer-focused, and when the customer has experienced less than stellar service from some other part of your organization, it's tempting, very tempting, to want to jump up and do battle for the customer, to say to the customer, "They can't treat you like that—I won't let them." It feels good, being the hero for your customer. But when you cast your company as villain, nobody wins.

"I'm so stupid."

We all do things that can be categorized as "dumb." Slamming one's finger in the cash register comes to mind. So too does blurting out something inappropriate to the customer—"Yes, Mrs. Duck, you can just waddle on back and see her." Customers do dumb things as well. And being good service professionals, we often want to help them out. It's called the rescue syndrome. When customers realize they've done something foolish, there are two typical responses. The first is to distance themselves from the action—"I may have been dumb, but it's still all your fault!" Much more pleasant but far trickier to deal with is the second customer response—asking for assistance. It's the, "I'm so dumb, but you'll help me anyway, won't you?" plea. It's a tough question to answer because it *seems* so easy.

Jerry Brill, a young bank officer we met in a seminar, tells of his first encounter with an "I'm so stupid" customer:

> She was the classic little old lady in tennis shoes. There she stood, checkbook and statement in hand. "I'm so bad at math, could you help me?!" she begged. It was a slow afternoon, so I said, "Sure," and had her in balance in about twenty minutes. The next month, the day after the statements went out, there she was. Checkbook and statement in hand. "Yoo-hoo! I'm back, Mr. Brill." It took me six months to teach her to balance her own statements.

Jerry's customer was a classic example of:

"I'm so stupid. Did you ever see such a dumb mistake?!"

Our partner Chip Bell says that in these situations "the goal is not to help the customer feel better about being weak. The goal is to help the customer become strong." The most effective way to work with an "I'm so stupid" customer is to *rebuild the self-reliance he or she seems to have lost.* Avoid using the word "mistake" when talking with your customer about the problem. This may be an opportunity for you to conduct some customer education. Jerry's initial response should have been something like:

> *"I've done the same thing myself. It's easy to get confused. Let me show you how I remember."*

Variation 1: "I don't think I'm dying, but could you check?"

There are times when a customer's "I know I'm just being dumb" plea masks fear, not dependence or confusion. Your pat answer needs to *make the customer feel comfortable* about telling you what he or she has done, what he or she is thinking, how he or she feels, and what he or she wants or needs from you. Make the customer feel welcome and secure.

> **"I'm one of Dr. Ogle's more-than-a-little paranoid patients. Could I get you to squeeze me in for an appointment tomorrow or early the next day?"**

> *"We don't have any paranoid patients. We have patients with legitimate concerns. What prompted your call today?"*

Variation 2: "Can you rescue my cat from the tree?"

There are times when customers don't know they are being less than bright about a situation. *Keep the secret,* and *treat them with respect.* If later the customer figures it out, they'll save face with the thought "At least the service provider didn't realize I was acting so silly." And if customers never figure it out, well, that's okay, too. The case of the confused HMO caller who asked, "Aren't urology and neurology the same except for the spelling?" comes quickly to mind.

Not too long ago we worked with a terrific crew of 911 dispatchers. As you know, this life-saving service is designed to handle the most critical of human emergency calls—crime in progress, threat to human life, officer needing assistance. But, as you might suspect, not every call that comes into a 911 line fits that description. Yet all dispatchers know that if you alienate a citizen because one particular call isn't a true emergency, that citizen may not call back when there is a legitimate, life-endangering emergency. The dispatcher's solution: Treat the caller with respect and offer all possible assistance, while treating him or her to a little live action sound from "real emergencies."

> **"Is this 911? My kitty is caught in a tree. Send someone out right away—I just don't know what to do!"**

"Are there any people in danger? (Siren: Whoop! Whoop!) *I'm sorry, I'm dispatching an ambulance. We are the first call for crimes in progress, suspicious behavior, and medical emergencies. Hold please* (several seconds pass). *Please call the Humane Society for your kitty—the number is 555–5555, and thank you for keeping 911 by your phone."*

One other note about 911 service. Dispatchers must constantly and quickly switch between voice and radio communication. Clear radio communication requires a neutral tone of voice, one with little vocal inflection. If you find yourself using a walkie-talkie with customers or coworkers, keep your vocal tone flat and comprehension of what you've said will increase.

"Are you saved?"

Pick up just about any guide to business etiquette and you'll find an admonition to eschew talk of religion and politics in the workplace. They are topics about which convictions are deeply held and a middle ground is not always easy to find. So, by mutual consent we avoid raising the subject—it's an unspoken social contract designed to smooth the waters of daily conversation, especially in work settings where we generally don't feel as free to express our personal views. Yet we've all spoken with customers—and friends—on the phone or in person who have political, religious, or other convictions they like to "share" with others regardless of time or place. They make comments or ask questions that seem to be right out of left field, but they feel free to blurt them out, nonetheless. And they frequently expect that we will be grateful for their insight and concern. In your personal life, you may feel free to agree or disagree with others' opinions. But on the job, when the focus is on serving customers, disagreeing is risky and agreeing can land you in the middle of an extended conversation that is irrelevant to your service task. You may even feel a bit annoyed that the customer put you on the spot. So, how can you find a way out when presented with comments and questions about religion, politics or other vital issues of the day?

When the issue is religion, your simplest tactic is to *assume the best of intentions and redirect the conversation*. Leave aside the issue of "appropriateness" for a moment. For the sake of customer service, you can acknowledge the good intentions, without acknowledging the religious view behind them or encouraging further conversation. Your goal is to "close" the discussion and redirect the conversation to an appropriate topic as quickly and as simply as possible. Here's a response we've seen work well:

"Are you saved?"

"Thank you. How might I help you today?"

The same principle works when the patter turns to politics. Most of us would affirm or correct a friend's political views, but the customer is, well, still the customer. Your answer should not agree, insult, or make an issue out of anything. Just redirect the conversation and move on. Our favorite example:

"I can't understand why anyone would have voted that clown into office, can you?"

"That's politics. How may I help you today?"

We are not suggesting that difficult issues and personally held values never have a place in our work-a-day lives. Rather, we need to recognize and address the fact that they have a tremendous potential for distracting us from providing Knock Your Socks Off Service.

Three Helpful Phrases For All Occasions

In our work, we've come across three phrases so helpful they deserve a chapter of their own. We heard them from many different service professionals working with many different types of customers. They can be used time and time again, in situation after situation, to smooth the way.

Helpful Phrase #1: "As you might expect"

This little gem suggests that you and your customer share a worldview. It puts you both on the same side of the fence. It also allows you to share information with the customer, while suggesting "I know that you already know this."

> "As you might expect, *there is an awful lot of paperwork with any government-funded project.*"

> "As you might expect, *we have many policies designed to ensure the privacy of our customer's records. That's why the signed waiver form is required.*"

Helpful Phrase #2: ". . . *for you*"

In these two words lies magic. Their power is surprising. They tell the customer, "I'm here on *your* behalf, *you* are in control, and *you* are at the core of my concern." These words increase cooperation and decrease frustration.

"Just a moment while I pull up that credit record for you."

"That's a good question. Let me find out for you."

Helpful Phrase #3: "This *account* shows" or "*Our records* indicate"

It's all too easy for customers to get defensive, especially when late payment or failed commitments are at issue. We have seen collections agents and mortgage clerks alike build rapport—and cooperation—with customers by separating the person from the debt. Call a customer and begin with, "You owe . . ." and you'll get very little in return. Change the focus to the forms and the records:

> *"Ms. Customer, this account shows a past due balance of $197.04. Does that agree with your records?"*

Or this variation from a mortgage company:

> *"I've been reviewing the file for your application, and our records indicate that the confirmation of employment and salary forms are missing. I'll need your help to get that into the file."*

If you have a helpful phrase, one that has served you time and time again, we invite you to send it to us so we can share it with other service professionals. Send your phrase, along with your name and address, and we'll send you a Knock Your Socks Off Service® button:

Knock Your Socks Off Answers
PO Box 582569
Minneapolis, MN 55408

Twenty Things You Should Never Say to a Customer

We all know there are some things you just *never* say to customers, words and phrases that provoke the worst sort of reaction. But even if you are the most careful person in the room, the occasional customer will catch you unaware, and you will end up saying something that you didn't intend.

Here are twenty words and phrases that seem to send customers into spasms and fits of pique. Photocopy them at 140 percent on your copy machine and post them near your phone or counter. Maybe—no guarantee—but maybe the presence of this list will save you the need for several hours of apology and explanation over the next year.

Twenty Things You Should Never Say to a Customer

"#$!!!#$"
"She's out of the state."
"Aren't you through yet?"
"It sure took you long enough!"
"You whine just like my in-laws."
"She went to buy another candy bar."
"Of course he has my number—I'm returning his call."
"He stepped out and took the *Wall Street Journal* with him."
"Aren't you the lady that called with that really dumb question?"
"If you'll start sounding like an adult and not a two-year-old . . ."
"Well, I never heard of anything like that before."
"Too bad. Better luck next time."
"I can't do that. Our policy is . . ."
"Sir, that's just not possible."
"Ya, well, so what?"
"You'll have to . . ."
"It's not my job."
"I don't know."
"Little lady."
"Dude."

From *Knock Your Socks Off Answers* by Kristin Anderson and Ron Zemke (New York: AMACOM, 1995).

Part 2

Smart Answers to Even Tougher Questions

In quarreling the truth is always lost.

Publilius Syrus
First century B.C.

The secret is to understand the customer's problems, and provide solutions so as to help that customer be profitable and feel good about the transaction.

Francis (Buck) Rodgers
Retired IBM sales guru

I can evade questions without help; what I need is answers.

John F. Kennedy

Just about the time you finally learn all the answers, they change all the questions.

Anonymous

Sometimes the question the customer asks or the objection he raises makes a lot of sense, is right on the mark, is well intended—and is very difficult to answer both *well* and tactfully. When the customer asks:

"What time is the 3 o'clock show?"

it takes great restraint to avoid the obvious and smart-alecky

"Oh, I don't know, would 3 o'clock be a good guess?"

and answer the real question the customer is trying, unsuccessfully, to ask.

In the same vein, there are customer questions and complaints that are real to the customer but that are based on a very bad misunderstanding of the way things work in your world:

"Now look here. My pension checks are due the first and the fifteenth. I know that you purposely hold them over the weekends just so you can make money on the float!"

The customers' interests in these examples have nothing to do with the question asked or the accusation made. In the former, the customer wants to know when to arrive for the 3 o'clock show; in the latter, the customer wants to know why his checks aren't arriving on the dates he expects them. The right answers have to answer the question, be understandable to the customer, and respect the customer as a customer. It's a nifty little tightrope every customer service person must learn to walk. Consider this section a helpful net.

"You're wrong. I ordered the small, not the large."

Customers are as honest as the day is long, at least most of them. Most of the time. You know that. We know that. And there is even research that purports to prove what your and our experience has taught us. Customers are not, however, always correct. And neither are we. Everyone makes mistakes, gives wrong information, misunderstands instructions, or simply perceives a situation in a "unique" or "idiosyncratic" way—at least some of the time. What we believe we've said and what customers say they heard are not always the same.

And vice versa. That is the nature of communication, even between people who've lived together for twenty years.

You can't win an argument about a misunderstanding or a misspeak. Even if you can prove who was wrong and who was right, you lose. So don't even try. Besides, your goal is to keep the customer coming back, not to decide who's right and who's wrong. That doesn't mean you should blindly believe "the customer is always right" or that you are always wrong when you see things differently from the customer. Rather, it means looking for ways to turn a wrong customer into a right customer—one who will continue to do business with you.

There are two thoughts to keep in mind when you hear the following:

"You're wrong. I ordered the small, not the large."

First, you want to keep the customer from becoming defensive—or if the customer already is, to defuse that defensiveness. Second, you want to get past the knee-jerk desire to "fix the blame" on someone and start solving the problem. At a moment in time when you and the customer are seeing the world in very different ways, blame is almost always irrelevant.

To meet these goals, the simplest, most useful, and, in the long run, most cost-effective response is to *believe the customer*. Treat the 1 percent of "questionable" customers as if they were honest rather than treating the 99 percent of honest customers with suspicion. A fast-food restaurant chain we are familiar with found it wasn't worth an employee's time to argue over the size beverage the customer ordered. Instead, it advocates a simple policy—"Don't fight. Make it right."

"I'm sorry. I'll make sure you are only charged for the small."

Variation 1: "You ruined my son's birthday."

Believing the customer without question may be the easiest way to go when the product is a fountain beverage or box of popcorn. There are other times, however, when the dollar amount in dispute is more substantial or the customer's charge of "You're wrong" is tied to an accusation of corporate wrongdoing—times when the customer believes he or she was tricked into accepting a particular service or shipped products that were not ordered. In situations where you cannot or are not allowed simply to give in to the customer's point of view, a three-step approach will help you create your best response.

Step 1. *Apologize for the customer's upset.* Your apology here is not an acceptance of blame. Rather, it is an *acknowledgment* of the customer's emotional state and inconvenience. Sometimes your acknowledgment will immediately cause your customer to cool down.

> **"I'm sorry the new bike you bought for your son was broken on his birthday. That must have been very disappointing for both of you."**

Step 2. *Find some point on which you both can agree.* Without a common starting point, you and your customer will be locked in an argument without end. Your point of agreement will help you gain customer cooperation in working toward a final resolution or understanding.

> **"I agree. A bike should last. I'm very concerned that your son's bike didn't. I want to get this situation corrected so that you and your son can go biking again very soon. Thank you for bringing the bike in with you. That's a real help."**

Step 3. *Probe for more information.* Try to understand what happened, when, and to whom. Don't worry about the "why" of the misunderstanding at this point. Ask questions like "Tell me more about that" or "Walk me through exactly what happened." By the way, sometimes the customer's explanation of what happened doesn't make sense or seems technically impossible—"The butter caused my microwave to make a shower of sparks" or "It must have turned itself on and burned the motor out." Remember: The customer generally doesn't have your technical expertise and background, but that doesn't negate his or her perception of the situation or need for your help.

If you have information the customer may not have, share

it. This exchange of information should help clarify the situation and allow the mistaken party—you or your customer—to save face when the cause of the misunderstanding is finally discovered. Note: The less like an interrogation your conversation is, the easier it will be for one of you to say "Oops! I guess I was wrong."

Consider an example we overheard in a discussion between a subscription clerk for a popular trade magazine and a confused customer.

Customer:	I never ordered this magazine. Are you people trying to trick me into subscribing?
Subscription Clerk:	Oh, certainly not. I'm sorry if there's been some mix-up. We certainly don't want to send our publication out to people who don't want it, just as I'm sure you don't want to receive magazines you didn't order. If I can ask you just a couple of questions, I will be able to straighten this out for you. First, is there a code on the upper left corner of the mailing label? Can you read it to me?
Customer:	O465 PSP.
Subscription Clerk:	Great. (Pause) Okay, I see that our records show that the subscription was entered into our system by Debbie on the day after Labor Day based on a telephone conversation with a person named Todd.
Customer:	Todd? I just let go an employee named Todd. I am beginning to see what may have happened.
Subscription Clerk:	Would you like me to cancel the subscription for you?
Customer:	Yes. And thank you for helping me figure out just what did happen.

Variation 2: "Don't tell me it doesn't exist! I know it does!"

There are times when the customer is dead wrong or, at the very least, mistaken, and upset to boot. It is tempting to try to reeducate the customer, to help her see the error of her ways, in hopes that the "truth" will calm her down. Big mistake! You are more than likely to create a situation that needs to be defused by a third party—another service representative, your boss, your boss's boss—somebody who isn't you.

We watched this play out elegantly on the sales floor of a computer software retail store. Bob, a computer salesperson, was faced with a customer who insisted, "Windows version 6.0 allows you to transfer files between a Mac and a PC." Bob tried to explain that there was no Windows 6.0. After all, he ought to know; he sells the stuff. But the customer continued to insist, "It exists. I use it every day at work." It was an argument Bob couldn't win even though he was right. Fortunately, a colleague, Samantha, intervened before the argument got out of hand.

Samantha: I'm sorry there seems to be some confusion here. Perhaps I can be of assistance.

Customer: I'm trying to buy the Windows 6.0 that allows you to transfer files between Mac and PC. I use it at work. I know it exists.

Samantha: Microsoft™ does have a Windows-based processing program that allows you to do that. It's called Word™ 6.0. Is that what you use at work?

Customer: Yes, that's it exactly.

Samantha: Bob will be able to help you find that. Bob?

Bob: I'm sorry for the confusion. Let me show you where the Word software is kept.

Samantha helped Bob back off, gain some composure, and apologize. She then found a point of agreement and used it as a starting point and led the customer to the right product. The clue to the "reality" of this customer's need was there all the time. Bob was just too caught up in being right to see it. Give your customer the benefit of the doubt—and be willing to ask for help when at loggerheads with a customer over a "fact"—and you will benefit, too.

"I was here first. Why are you helping her?"

According to a study by Fortino & Associates, a San Francisco-based research firm, the average American spends five years of his or her life waiting in line. Customers wait for movie tickets and buses, telephones to be answered, and products to arrive by mail. It's no wonder customers have developed little internal alarm clocks that tell them when they've waited long enough and when it ought to be their turn. Try to cheat them of that cherished moment, and customers will loudly proclaim, "No butting in line; I was here first." Customers look to the service provider to ensure fair treatment for all. At the first sign that another customer may be receiving special treatment—served out of order or allowed to skip the waiting lines—customers will hold your feet to the fire of their upset with some pointed and barely civil version of:

"Excuse me. I was here first. Why are you helping her?"

Your best bet: Work to *avoid or prevent the situation* before it begins. A hotel chain we worked with found it could significantly decrease the number of complaints about waiting in line during check-in by making sure all desk receptionists practiced this simple routine:

1. Make eye contact with waiting guests.
2. Verbally acknowledge the guest's presence.
3. Promise the guest attention soon.
4. When the guest reaches the front of the queue, thank him or her for being so patient, whether the guest was patient or not.

Often it's not the waiting itself that is the annoyance; it's not knowing how long the wait will be. You reduce customer fretting when you answer the question "Why are you helping her? I was here first" with:

> *"I'm sorry. I will be finished with this transaction in just a few moments and then I will be right with you. Thank you for being so patient."*

When you're finally face to face with the customer and it's obvious the customer is upset, your best course of action is to *apologize immediately* for the wait. Then do what you can to remedy the situation. This happens frequently when a number system is used to determine order of service. Invariably the customer clutching Number 44 wanders out of earshot for the brief moment when Number 44 is being called and an overzealous Number 45 rushes up and gushes, "I guess there's no Number 44, so I'm next." By the time Number 44 wanders back, you are in the middle of handling Number 45, and it's too late to stop. However, it's not too late for a Smart Answer:

> *"And your number is? 44? Oh, I am sorry your number was missed. Thank you for letting me know. Please allow me to help you next. All right?"*

Other times what a customer perceives as "unfair" and "line butting" may indeed be *your* effort to make things more fair.

> *"I understand you've been waiting in line. This customer was here earlier and I asked him to come back to the front of the line. I will be with you in just a moment. Thank you."*

With so much time spent waiting, it's no wonder customers have become extremely sensitive to wait time and have come to equate "quick" with "quality." Acknowledging the importance of your customers' time and dealing with the upset that waiting may cause will help prove to your customers that you always have their needs in mind.

"Do you have a brain, or what?!"

Everyone wants respect. Turn-of-the-century psychologist William James said, "The deepest principle of human nature is a longing to be appreciated." In street slang, no one likes being "dissed" or "treated with disrespect." This is true of you, us, your customers, your kids, and everyone you and we know. It may not be a constitutional right, but it is clearly a social obligation.

Just the same, there are times and frustrations that cause customers to forget this simple fact of life. When upset, frustrated, and fearful that the problem won't be resolved, the customer will lash out at the nearest person—you:

"LET ME REPEAT THIS SLOWLY AND CLEARLY, IN ONE-SYLLABLE WORDS THAT EVEN YOU CAN UNDERSTAND."

Some customers can convey that same sentiment—without words. You start to answer the customer's question or complaint and she rolls her eyes, shakes her head, looks at the floor, pays no attention to you, and without uttering a single word conveys the message:

"Do you have a brain, or what?!"

Don't reach for a cream pie—or a hammer. If you respond to the insult in any way, neither you nor your customer will ever get back to the real issue. This disrespectful customer is frustrated. The frustration may be with your organization's policies, procedures, and systems. It may even be with her own mistakes or simply with life in general.

Your best bet: *Do not assume that every insulting, mean-acting customer is a Customer From Hell*℠—just assume that he or she is upset. Period. Employees at theme parks like Walt Disney World, Magic Mountain, and Six Flags are encouraged to think about the jobs they perform as roles, parts in a play, rather than as expressions of their own persona. Upset customers usually are upset with your role or the organization for which you play a role; they are very seldom upset with you personally.

We've found that negative customer behavior often occurs when customers feel the situation slipping out of their control. Acknowledge their frustration and put them back in control by *asking for assistance with a task.*

> *"I can see this is frustrating for you—it is for me, too. Please give me a moment to pull up the order record for you. While I am working on this, could you doublecheck these papers to make sure we have your company information and ship-to address down correctly?"*

If the customer refuses to work with you and seems to be making a personal attack on you, *call a time out*—a break in the action that stops everything from escalating and gives both you and your customer a chance to calm down and reevaluate. It is perfectly acceptable for you to tell a customer:

"This is more complex than I thought. I'm going to need about twenty-five minutes to work on it. I don't want to tie you up while I check everything. You are welcome to wait here or I can call you at your office within thirty minutes. Which would you prefer?"

Throughout this trying transaction, remain cool, calm, collected, and very straight-faced. No head shaking, jaw clenching, or eyeball rolling on your part. When you act upset, when you do the behaviors upset people do, you run the risk of actually *becoming* upset. You can't afford the luxury of making yourself upset every time a customer flies off the handle at you. In some service jobs you'd burn out in a day. Remaining calm will show your competence and skill far more effectively than rising to the bait and shouting back, "Yes, I do have a brain, and feelings . . . unlike some of my customers!"

"Sorry, hell!
Do something!"

When something goes wrong, the first thing customers should hear is a simple, heartfelt "Gee, I'm really sorry about that." Your apology is your acknowledgment of the upset and inconvenience. By itself, of course, "I'm sorry" is not enough. It *must* be a prelude to problem solving. Unfortunately, too many customers have heard "I'm sorry" without ever seeing any action. If you don't take corrective steps quickly, in a way that is *visible* to customers, their anger and frustration will increase. And understandably so. Empathy without action isn't good enough. Customers who perceive that the apology is all they are going to get are the customers most prone to blurting out:

"Sorry, hell! Do something!"

Your best response is to ignore the anger in their vocal tone and words and to *demonstrate action.* Through your body language, your vocal tone, and your facial expression, show you are concerned. It's a little piece of theater in which customers place a great amount of stock. Your work pace and level of emotion should remain controlled. Panic and uncertainty are the last things the customer needs, or wants, to see. Show and tell the customer exactly what you have done and what you will do next to address the situation. During this process, you may make promises to the customer. When you do, promise *actions*, not *outcomes*. It's tempting to promise results such as "I will have everything fixed within the next twenty minutes," but the outcome, or final resolution, may be outside your control. Actions, on the other hand, are within your control and each action you take can show the customer that you are working on his or her behalf. Every promise you make should be written down. That will give you an opportunity to track your own performance. Keep a paper trail to document your work for future reference.

The exact words you say, the actions you promise and demonstrate, will depend on the specific situation the customer presents. An HMO member services representative might handle a member's call to "do something" about a surgery bill sent directly to the member by saying:

> *"I've pulled up your records for you on my system and I don't see any notation that we've received the bill for your surgical procedure from the hospital. I've entered all of the information you gave me and as soon as we hang up, I'm going to call the surgical clinic to find out why the bill was sent to you 'payment due in full.' As soon as I talk with them and get some answers, I'll call you back. It may be a day or two; will that be okay?"*

Suppose your company supplies parts to a major manufacturer, and last week a traincar-load of parts was destroyed en route to a customer. This customer's Greenville manufacturing facility will have to shut down, costing your customer hundreds of thousands of dollars, unless you are somehow able to replace the destroyed shipment. In a situation like this one, your plans and actions will be highly complex. Reporting on the details of what is happening tells your customer you are working on the problem and are leaving no stone unturned in your search for a solution:

> *Mr. Smith, I'm calling to tell you what I've done so far. As you know, the immediate goal is to get 10,000 units shipped to your Greenville facility. I've placed priority calls to all of our warehouse facilities and expect to hear back from them within the hour. I am also checking with two of our other clients who use the units to see if we can 'borrow' product from them. I should have some concrete information to report to you by 4 P.M. today. I will call you at that time. Will you be*

in your office then, or is there a beeper or car phone number I should have?"

In situations where your customer's world is falling apart, it is only natural for him or her to look for ways to regain control. At these moments, customers don't want empathy as much as they want action. A caution: When the customer is really worried and upset, nothing you do is going to make him or her "happy." If you judge your own success on your ability to create a smile on this customer's face, you will be disappointed. Smiles and words of appreciation for your efforts will come, but they will come days, weeks, sometimes even months later. It will take time for your customer to feel back in balance and safe.

"What do I want to have happen? I'm going to tell you exactly what WILL happen. First, you're going to. . . ."

We've said it several times already, and we'll say it again: Perceived loss of control creates fear in the hearts and minds of customers—fear that the problem will never be solved, fear that the situation is going to cost the customer time and/or money, fear that the customer will lose face, fear that the customer will be blamed. Some customers will throw themselves on your mercy and expect you to solve all their woes, like a surrogate mom or dad. Some customers respond to fear with anger, upset, and even insult. Others respond by seizing control and ordering people—*you*—around:

"What do I want to have happen? I'm going to tell you exactly what WILL happen. First, you're going to. . . ."

Attitude and unsavory behavior aside, the customer's "suggestion" may in fact have merit, may even be the very thing you were *already* going to do. In that case, chalk this one up as a service success and *follow directions*.

"That's a great idea—I can do that for you!"

In other situations, giving orders—any orders—is the customer's way of lashing out, especially since those orders often involve something you couldn't do even if you wanted to. Contradicting your customer's orders with a direct statement such as "I can't do that" or "That would never work; it's impossible" will only lead you into a very ugly argument.

Your best bet: *Redirect* the customer. He is focused on his solution—workable or not. You need to redirect him back to his real need. Then you will be able to offer alternative suggestions that will work. A favorite travel agency of ours offers this sample response to a customer who insisted that the agent close her office and hand-deliver the needed tickets.

> *"I understand your primary concern is having the ticket ready and waiting for you at the airport, without having to depend on a ticket delivery service. I can process a prepaid ticket for you that will be waiting at the airline check-in counter. There is a twenty-dollar charge for that service, which I can take care of through your regular billing. Okay?"*

It's tempting to tell these dictatorial customers just how much they don't know, to provide them with a little learning for the future—"You know, that wouldn't happen if you would just. . . ." You can't educate the irate. Angry, order-shouting customers are not in a "teachable moment." They won't listen and will resent the effort. Remember, and we *know* we are repeating ourselves, when you hear or sense anger or frustration, save your words of wisdom for another time.

"What time is the three o'clock show?"

Kathy Ridge, a friend of ours in Charlotte, North Carolina, spent a long hot summer during her college years at Paramount's Carawinds theme park standing in front of a board listing special event times and answering the question:

"What time is the three o'clock show?"

She says that the first day it took every ounce of will power she possessed not to respond with "It's at 3:00! You dummy!" Gradually, Kathy realized, "What time is the three o'clock show?" wasn't the real question. Park guests were really asking different questions from the one she thought she was hearing—questions that ranged from, "Will it start on time?" and "How early do we need to arrive to get good seats?" to "What are our options if we can't make it at three o'clock?" Kathy ended her frustration by creating a more complete response:

"The show will start promptly at three o'clock, so you'll want to arrive at least fifteen minutes early to get the best seats."

We all have stories like Kathy's about customers who ask questions that are, on their face, absurd, stupid, and almost unbelievable. Like Kathy, we need to learn to listen for the important question lurking beneath the obvious, odd, or even silly sounding one.

In most situations, your customers are simply not asking the question they really want answered. There is a legitimate question or request, but the customer simply doesn't know how to word it. A retired hair stylist we know loves to tell about a little girl who came into her shop the day before the start of school. The little girl was the victim of a kitchen table haircut. With tears in her eyes she asked, "Mrs. Resell, please, can you cut my bangs longer?" Her request was not for information but for understanding. Our friend's response was a confident:

> *"Sure, honey, I can cut your bangs longer! I'll just pull some more hair forward and give those short wisps a chance to grow out."*

The girl and her mother were good customers for years after that.

Variation 1: "Are the fish biting yet?"

Sometimes the question itself is reasonable and understandable—but you haven't a ghost of an answer. In these cases, your best course of action is to *direct the customer to a more appropriate resource.* Consider the customer service representatives of a western power company. Every year they can count on several calls from citizens asking, "What kind of fish are in the reservoir? And what are they biting on?" Rather than take on a role for which they have no expertise, they've created a response that directs the caller to a better source of information without offending:

> *"Good question! The reservoir ecosystem is managed by the state Department of Natural Resources. I happen to have their number right here. They should be able to help you. Hope you catch a big one!"*

Variation 2: "Lens cap? What lens cap?"

There are still other situations where the question reveals a gap in the customer's knowledge about your product or service. We make assumptions—often, wrong assumptions—about how much our customers already know and understand about using our products and services. So when we hear a question about something we think of as common knowledge, we should recognize it as an opportunity to provide a little customer education—provided, of course, that the customer isn't too upset to be in a teachable moment. A common situation in the photo processing business is the "red-eyes syndrome." Some customers insist, "You must have processed the film wrong!" when they see red dots where their children's pupils should be. Instead of dismissing such customers as obvious amateurs, smart photo professionals say something like:

> *"Hmm, may I take a look at those? You're right, the eyes are definitely red. What type of camera are you using? I see. I think I can explain what's happening to cause this—it's not a processing issue. There is a simple trick I use to fix the red-eye thing when it happens to my pictures. I just take a black felt-tip pen and. . . ."*

Regardless of the situation, your goal is to help the customer feel good about asking the question, even if it seems silly or strange. Customers need to feel that as far as you are concerned, there is no such thing as a stupid question. You make them feel that way when you take all their questions seriously. If you laugh at customers' "silly" or "odd" questions, they'll stop asking any questions at all—including questions like "Can you sell me a whole lot of your best, most expensive products and services?"

"But can't you just push a button?"

Technology today is so advanced that in many instances yesterday's miraculous is today's ordinary. Think about the technology we have in our homes—the telephone, 500-channel TVs with direct satellite connections, utility meters that call in their own readings, computer chips programmed to maintain an optimal temperature for specific times of the day and customized for every room in the house. The questions we ask today are no longer "Will it ever be possible to?" but rather, "When will I be able to buy this?" Most people don't know or even wonder how all these modern miracles work. They just plug them in, turn them on, and go.

That attitude, what we call "technomysticism," can make it difficult to provide good service for these cutting-edge, complex products. Because technology has moved or broken so many limits, customers see our offerings and capabilities as practically limitless. When we have to tell customers our technology *can't* do something, they more often than not respond with a plaintive:

"But can't you just push a button? You know, like they do on 'Star Trek'?"

Your best bet: When responding to questions based in technomysticism, stop and carefully *explode the myths* your customer is clinging to.

Consider the case of a market research company with which we're familiar. Complicated statistical data analysis is run on its mini-mainframe computer system. Its customers are quite blasé about the computing and data-crunching miracles the company routinely delivers. Just the same, sales and service people at the company work hard to be sure that customers understand that technology is a tool, with limits and strengths just like any other tool. For all that, however, the company still has customers who *want* the technomystical experience—they don't want to understand the tools. They want dark miracles.

The market research firm's project coordinators use a simple three-step approach to deal with their customers' yearning for the technomystical:

Step 1: They *acknowledge the customer's request* in a positive way. Says one project coordinator, "I used to get mad sometimes that they even asked—didn't they know it wasn't that easy? Then I realized that my customers often don't know what's involved in fulfilling their requests. And in any case, they have every right to ask for whatever they want. It's my job to respect those requests and ensure my customers get what they need."

Step 2: They briefly *explain the technology*. If the request is impossible, they say so and why. If it is possible but not necessarily easy or desirable, they give the customer a general idea of the amount of effort involved, using measures such as person work hours, time, impact on other areas, and cost.

Step 3: If the customer still wants it, they *investigate how it might be delivered* at a reasonable cost.

For example, a client asked Stephanie, a project coordinator, to run an analysis of customer survey data by size of the respondents' home towns—the cities in which the respondents were born. Although an open-ended question asked each respondent for the name of his or her home town, no data about town size was collected at the time of the interview.

Client: Can't you just feed in an almanac or something and push a button and have it all just pop out?

Stephanie: I can understand why that would be interesting data to have. It would be possible to do. Let's look at what would be involved. First, we would need to decide if we wanted to use the current population size or the size of the town at the time the respondent was born. We would then need to create a data table of all the home towns

mentioned by respondents, the years of the respondents' birth, and the population of the towns
at that time. That would mean examining over
1,500 respondent files. As you might expect, that
will get time- and labor-intensive and significantly add to the cost of the project. But we
could do it.

Client: It was really just a passing thought. Let's not do it
this time.

It didn't take very much discussion before this client realized the request wasn't worth the effort. Letting the customer
have the final say leaves the customer's sense of control intact.

"Hello, hello? Can't I talk to a real person?"

In a survey of U.S. executives, the Menlo Park, California-based temporary employee agency Accountemps found that 40 percent of respondents believe voice mail systems are annoying and/or hard to use. According to another survey, this one by U.S. Message Corporation, up to 30 percent of callers hang up when they encounter automated telephone response systems. In short, many customers resent the way some companies use high technology as a low-fidelity substitute for human contact. And they let them know about it, too, from "No, you may not put me into her voice mail" to "I've been stuck in your telephone system for what seems like hours!" to this plaintive message left on more than one call answering system:

"Hello, Hello? Can't I talk to a real person?"

Voice mail, and all of its automated voice-processing cousins, is here to stay. With time and better implementation, acceptance is growing. Just consider the home answering machine. We all know people who swore they would never have one but now can't live without theirs. The challenge is to respond well to the frustration and confusion your system may from time to time cause for your customers.

Your best bet: *Test your system.* If it is causing concern and consternation, it may not be working as it was programmed to do. A member services representative at an HMO we worked with noticed an upswing in customer complaints about not getting through to a real person and being disconnected while going through the "For questions about your policy, press 1" menu. She called into the system herself and discovered that it was indeed malfunctioning. She then called to alert the telecommunications coordinator, and the problem was corrected that same day. While the telecommunications staff was working to correct the problem, member services representatives were able to assure customers that their negative experience was an exception, not the rule.

> *"Thank you so much for your patience. And I apologize for the inconvenience our system caused you. We are experiencing a temporary glitch in our voice-processing system. It should be corrected shortly. How might I assist you today?"*

Whenever possible, *make voice mail an option, not a demand.* A company we regularly call has a human on the switchboard who gives callers the option of using voice mail or of leaving a message with her.

Educate customers about the best ways to use your system. For example, many newspapers now offer a voice-mail system subscribers can use to temporarily suspend home delivery, such as when the customer will be out of town for a few days. Subscribers who call during regular business hours and speak to a live subscription representative are coached on using the voice-mail system the next time.

> *"There, I have your delivery canceled from the twenty-fourth through the twenty-ninth. You know, we have a special phone service for stops and starts that you can use twenty-four hours a day. If you're like me and often think of these things late, the night before you're leaving on your trip, you can call 555-5555 and leave a voice message— our system will prompt you for all of the necessary information. Thanks for making us your paper! And have a great trip."*

Whatever you do, make certain there is an easy way for your customers to exit or avoid your automated system and reach a real person if they need or want to. Customer service is at its core a person-to-person affair. The harder we make it for that person-to-person transaction to occur, the harder we make it for our customers to do business with us. If you agree with this reasonable, rational point of view, press 2. If you do not agree, stay on the line. We'll get to you when we have a minute.

"How can I fill this out if I don't understand it?"

Paperwork—forms, statements, invoices—that make perfect sense to us and fit our business processes and systems may be unintelligible or confusing to customers. Just think for a moment about the forms we all fill out for the Internal Revenue Service. Although the IRS tries to make its forms and their instructions as simple as possible, most taxpayers approach them with a sense of dread. Forty percent of us even go so far as to pay someone else to fill them out for us.

While few businesses are as complicated as the IRS, confusion over forms and statements is still relatively common. It is rare that we encounter a form or statement so well designed that it is clearly understood by every customer who sees it. Front-line service professionals tell us they are frequently asked:

"How can I fill this out if I don't understand it?"

In these circumstances it's tempting to simply fill out the form for the customer—sometimes that seems to be the easiest, least time-consuming solution. For a one-time form for a one-time customer, that may be true. But beware; you may accidentally build a customer dependency you could come to regret. In order to determine your best course of action, you need first to determine whether the customer is genuinely puzzled or is simply resisting, and possibly resenting, being asked to fill out the paperwork. If the customer truly doesn't understand, your best bet is to *take the time to explain and clarify*. Make this an instructive act that leaves the customer feeling comfortable with the document.

"These mortgage application forms are quite lengthy. When I first saw them I thought they

looked more complicated than doing my taxes! But they really aren't that bad. Let me walk you through them."

As preparation for this kind of coaching, go through your most commonly used forms and note the parts that were confusing to *you* when you were new to your job or the form was first introduced. What do customers stop and ask questions about? Are there portions of the form that are frequently completed incorrectly or incompletely by customers?

Confusion exists not only in the forms we ask customers to fill out but in the statements we send to customers. A financial services company we've worked with completed a system-wide forms redesign in response to pleas from brokers and sales assistants for "statements that make sense to our clients." Even so, some of the brokers and financial planners went on to create their own statements, which they mail to their biggest and best accounts *along with* the standard company statement. These special statements were personally tailored to present information in the way that best met the needs of each individual customer. Yes, they did take time to create, but for these brokers, meeting the idiosyncratic needs of important key customers was well worth the effort.

"What do you mean by 'operator error'?"

John Goodman of the TARP organization, a customer research group in Washington, D.C., contends that customers cause at least a third of the problems they call on customer service professionals to fix. Because of that fact, it's tempting, during a problem resolution effort, to begin offering helpful observations:

> *"You know, if you weren't using the instruction manual to prop up that table leg, you might be able to find some of the correct command information on your own."*

Or:

> *"The Model 37 is a tough and sturdy disposal unit, but when people insist on putting things in it that don't belong, like Lego blocks, it isn't going to last very long."*

It's not surprising that customers react less than enthusiastically to these sorts of poorly veiled blaming suggestions. They may simply nod and smile. Or they may spit out an "Oh, really?" through clenched teeth. Or they may come straight out and challenge you with "What do you mean it isn't a machine problem?"

"What do you mean by 'operator error'?"

When you hear that phrase, or one like it, you are already in trouble. Your first step has to be to move backwards: *Stop, back up, and work on rebuilding the customer relationship.*

Make a statement to the customer that puts you both on

the same side of the fence, rather than nose to nose across some mythical battle line. Reassure the customer that you are not blaming him or her. Rather, your primary focus is on fixing the problem and preventing it from happening again.

> *"I've got kids myself and they once put every spoon we owned into the disposal at the same time. It took our dog a week to get over the shock of the noise that created."*

Your second step is to *take action to solve the immediate problem*. If possible, involve the customer in the solution process. One way to do this with equipment failure is to troubleshoot over the telephone or in person, explaining each activity to the customer as you go.

> *"There are any number of circumstances that can cause the printer error you experienced. Like you, I want to get that printer up and running as soon as possible. The quickest way for me to do that will be to troubleshoot it with you over the phone. I'll need your assistance with these tests; is that all right? Great!"*

In the final step, you may need to *provide some customer education*. Our colleague Chip Bell suggests educating through "personal discovery." Don't say, "You did this wrong and see what happened?!" Your customer will resent and resist your conclusions. Instead, outline the situation and the facts, then shut up and let the customer draw his or her own conclusion. It's a principle of human learning that we remember best the things we discover for ourselves.

Service Technician: According to the diagnostic we just completed, the printer and the computer are communicating without a problem when we print through DOS. But when we go into Windows we experience a problem. Can you think of any

	changes you've made recently to your computer or the way you use it?
Customer:	Well, I did load a new screen-saver program. I guess it never happened before I loaded that program.
Service Technician:	That could just be our problem.

Variation: "You've ruined my business— and my life."

There are situations wherein the cause of the error is obvious. Anyone who has repaired office equipment knows the joy of having to tell customers diplomatically that they forgot to plug the equipment into the power source or neglected to check whether their system was actually on line. Worse yet is having to explain to customers that the low-price bargain equipment they purchased through someone else has failed and caused the problem. But as careful as we plan to be in breaking this sort of news, there are customers who attack so quickly and forcefully that you don't get a chance to put your good intentions and fine skills into practice.

This was the situation a floral wholesaler we know faced with one of her customers, a small retail florist at the far edge of her service area. The customer had called twice to berate Lauren over a shipment of long-stemmed red roses that arrived two days later than promised. Lauren's investigation had found that the flowers left the wholesale greenhouse on time, but the contract carrier—the carrier specified by the customer—had failed to deliver on time.

But Jane at the retail store was having none of that explanation and refused Lauren's every effort at apology and compensation. Lauren was at her wit's end. Relying on clues picked up during months of unhappy telephone conversations, as well as her own years of experience, Lauren responded to Jane's fourth attacking phone call with a risky tactic. "Jane," she asked quietly, "what is it that you hate so much about running a floral shop?"

The question caught Jane off guard—and got beyond the

anger to Jane's real complaint. For the next forty tearful min-utes Jane poured out her soul to Lauren about how she'd left a career in nursing to open this business with a friend. Now the friend had bailed out and Jane was watching helplessly as her life savings dwindled away. Lauren spent another two hours counseling her customer on the rudiments of running a profit-able floral business and getting her connected to business support resources in her area.

With Jane's anger thus defused, Lauren went back to the original problem with a solution suggestion:

"How about this? As soon as I hang up, I can send you out a new order of long-stemmed red roses. I can send them by way of our preferred carrier. You should receive them before 10:30 A.M. tomor-row. Will that help?"

Yes, it was a big investment of Lauren's time, and a risk. But she wished she'd done it sooner: "It took less time, and caused less stress for me, than I'd already spent arguing with this customer. Our whole history of arguments about damaged shipments and carrier choices had everything to do with her frustrations and nothing to do with our performance. Once we cleared the air, our relations changed dramatically and to this day she is a very good customer." You are under no obligation to listen to the entire life story of every upset customer, but, as Lauren's story so clearly suggests, you can do a lot to mend an apparently torn customer relationship with a little patience, care, and understanding.

Part 3

Questions With No Easy Answers

Without tact you can learn nothing.
> Benjamin Disraeli
> 19th-century Prime Minister
> of Great Britain

Don't find a fault. Find a remedy.
> Henry Ford
> U.S. automobile manufacturer

Never say, "That's against company policy" unless you have a good explanation to back up the policy.
> Mary Kay Ash
> Founder of Mary Kay Cosmetics

The "silly question" is the first intimation of some totally new development.
> Alfred North Whitehead
> British mathematician and
> philosopher

No matter how innately witty, clever, well-schooled, calm, cool, and experienced you are, there are still customer questions that make you feel like Homer Simpson: "Duh! Why did he have to ask that!" Questions that make you want to wince and run away. And for good reason. There *are* questions customers ask that can't be answered to the customer's satisfaction. Questions that can't be answered from the rate card or the policy manual or that can't be passed off to someone "with more authority." They are questions with No Easy Answers. Sometimes they are questions and requests so odd as to be unique to that person, that time, that place. And you just make up the answer as you go along. Frequently these are what we call recovery situations; something has gone wrong and the customer needs us to set it right.

Sometimes the No Easy Answer question or request simply and plainly puts you between the customer and the company. You know exactly what the customer wants, what you should probably do; you also know that there is a policy absolutely forbidding you to do it. And a customer absolutely expecting—or at least hoping—that you will break that rule or ignore that policy.

There are, as the title of this section says, No Easy Answers to most of the questions in this section because the real answer to the question is all tied up in "It depends." What there *are* are ways of assessing the question or request to make it make sense. And ways to think about the possibility of breaking the rules. And ways to think about telling the customer "no." And ways to deal with those situations where the customer says, "Absolutely my way, or else!"

"I have a guaranteed reservation. What do you mean you gave my room away?"

Some of the toughest customer questions and situations revolve around an issue we call *service recovery*. Service recovery is what we do when things have been screwed up and we have to fix them for the customer. It may be that we, or our organization, made a mistake. Or it may be the customer who is in error. Or it even may be the result of a third-party failure—a vendor or supplier who didn't do his or her part—or an act of nature—a hurricane that toppled a tree onto the factory. Whatever the cause, these six steps to service recovery will serve you, and your customer, well:

1. Apologize/acknowledge the customer's inconvenience.
2. Listen, empathize, and ask open questions.
3. Fix the problem, quickly and fairly.
4. Offer atonement if the customer has been or feels "injured."
5. Keep the promises you make.
6. Follow up.

Consider how these steps played out for a print shop customer. When Nick handed Jill her order, she immediately saw that the fliers were printed on a heavy bond paper, not the slick paper she expected.

1. *Apologize/acknowledge the customer's inconvenience.* Upon realizing the problem, Nick said: "I am so sorry this happened."
2. *Listen, empathize, and ask open questions.* Nick learned how this situation was impacting the customer by listening and then asking Jill questions: "When did you need to first use these fliers?"
3. *Fix the problem, quickly and fairly.* Nick made a suggestion and asked for Jill's reaction: "Would it work to take these fliers with you to today's meeting? We will have the corrected fliers printed by tomorrow morning."
4. *Offer atonement if the customer has been or feels "injured."* Nick offered to pay for Jill's nonprinting expenses as a way of saying, "I want to make it up to you": "Since you came all the way over here, let me take care of your parking. I will also send someone over to your office with the corrected fliers so you don't have to make a second trip."
5. *Keep the promises you make.* Nick alerted his colleagues to the situation and the promises he had made to Jill. His team made certain that the correction was made and that the new fliers were promptly delivered.
6. *Follow up.* After the new fliers had been delivered, Nick called Jill: "Thank you again for alerting me to the situation. How do you like your new fliers?"

Nick used the six steps to solve what he hoped was an unexpected and one-time service problem. Other companies use the six steps to create effective responses to service and product breakdowns that they know will occur again and again, in spite of best efforts to prevent them. Consider the hotel industry. Guests who are expected to check out but who elect to stay on for another day may create a room shortage, resulting in another customer standing at the front desk, annoyed and angry.

Savvy front-desk employees use the six steps to manage the situation:

Customer: I have a guaranteed reservation. What do you mean you gave my room away?

Front-Desk Employee: I am so sorry, but we have an unexpected number of guests who've extended their stay with us.

Customer (interrupting) I just want to check into my room and relax. Then I've got a great deal of work to do tomorrow before driving to my client meeting.

Front-Desk Employee: I can certainly understand that, sir. I've already made an arrangement for you to stay at the Suites Hotel next door and will have one of our bell staff take you over and get you checked in. To make up for the inconvenience, I've put you on their executive level floor at our regular rate. That means a private lounge with free beverages and a buffet—it's a nice place to relax. Again, I really appreciate your working with us on this."

These six simple steps underlie our approach to answering questions and soothing situations for which there are no easy answers. For a more extensive explanation of service recovery, see *Delivering Knock Your Socks Off Service* (AMACOM, 1991).

"What do you mean that's not covered by the warranty?"

One of Murphy's laws promises that your toaster or TV will only break down *just after* the warranty has expired. There are customers who suspect that your company probably spends hundreds of hours and thousands of dollars making Murphy right by crafting carefully worded product warranties that remove any possibility of company liability for anything. Other customers are certain that even if the product is still within the warranty period, the retailer or dealer they bought the toaster or TV from will do everything possible to avoid any financial responsibility for the gone-bad product. Warranty issues can create frustration and ire in the most genteel customers.

Whether you work in a retail setting or for a manufacturer, warranty situations will come up. It's easy to feel caught in the middle between the company and the customer in these situations. The only way to avoid the squeeze is to be prepared to hear and respond to:

"What do you mean that's not covered by the warranty?"

before it ever comes up. That preparation takes a little homework.

Step 1: *Know your company's policy regarding warranties.* If your company's policies about warranties vary from product to product—for example, you work for a retail store that relies on the product manufacturer's warranty to determine refunds and exchanges—know the warranties for your best-selling products, or at least know where to go to quickly find out about them. If your company doesn't have a manual describing all of the major product warranties, create your own. A simple filing box or ring binder, alphabetized by product or manufacturer, can be a terrific place to keep copies of product warranties. And, of course, a computer file is the perfect place to store the details of warranty arrangements.

Step 2: *Ask around*. Ask your manager, your coworkers, anyone you can think of, these questions:

- Has our company made exceptions to the terms of product warranties in the past?
- Do exceptions to a warranty depend on the type of customer doing the asking, the customer's past history with our organization, the number of previous returns this customer has made, or other factors?
- Who gets to determine when exceptions to the warranty/ return policy may be made?"

Step 3: *Prepare an explanation of the warranty policy*. Write down the key points you will want to make when explaining the warranty to a customer. Try out your explanation in a practice session with coworkers. As you practice presenting your key points, think about the words and phrases you are using. Avoid saying, "It's our policy." Instead, say something like:

> **"Normally, our procedure is *to forward this type of product issue directly to the manufacturer. The manufacturer will then send you a check directly for the purchase price. In this case, however, I can simply do an even exchange* for you, *so everything will be taken care of today. How would that be?"***

Variation 1: "If you can't help me, who can?"

You may not be the person in your organization who gets to decide the legitimacy of a return. For some claims, the deciding person may not even be your manager or supervisor, but rather a representative from the manufacturer or supplier. Even when the decision of whether to accept or decline the return is not up to you, you can still play an important role between the customer and the company offering the warranty—suggesting approaches and making connections.

> *"Normally, we don't accept merchandise returns without a sales slip. There are a couple of things we could do. If you think the sales slip is at home, you could bring it and the toaster back with you another time. Or, you could contact the manufacturer directly for a replacement or refund—I can get the address for you. Or I could get our senior accounts person and see what she might suggest. What would work best for you?"*

Variation 2: "You expected me to do what?"

Some warranties have very strict requirements and obligations built into them. And, more often than not, your customers are only vaguely aware of them: "Of course I didn't keep the original box. I didn't expect this thing to quit working—did

you? You people said it's under warranty for a full year. How can you justify charging me twenty-five dollars just because I threw away the box?"

Your best response is to acknowledge the customer's upset and disappointment and *explain the rationale behind the policy*—if there is one. For example:

> *"I am sorry, but we ask our customers to retain the original box for the entire length of the warranty period so we can return the product to the manufacturer in the unlikely event that there is a problem. The twenty-five dollar fee covers our costs for returning the product without the original box."*

Even if customers disagree with the policy, they find *some* comfort in knowing that a reason exists for having the policy. But don't be surprised if they fail to thank you for the explanation.

"While you're at it, could you just . . . ?"

Customers frequently don't understand the time and effort that go into the work we do for them. Sometimes that's okay. We want our contributions to have a little "It would be my pleasure" mystique about them. Going the extra mile all the time is what has won the Nordstrom's department store chain its impressive customer loyalty and profitability. Extra added service is impressive—but there is a danger. If it becomes ordinary and expected, customers will no longer experience it as a delightful exception.

When the work we do looks effortless and easy to our customers, they may not value it. From a sales perspective, that means customers may resist paying for your expertise or assistance—after all, it was "no big deal" for you, so you shouldn't charge much, if anything. Customers may also believe that "because it's so easy, I should do it myself." Customers who find that they can't, in fact, do it themselves may blame you for the ensuing hassle and frustration.

Consider the plight of an independent lawn care and landscape expert of our acquaintance:

"While you're mowing the lawn, could you just stick these stakes in the ground where you think the sprinkler system should be installed? I can do the rest myself."

Your best bet: *Educate your customers about the work you do.* With knowledge comes appreciation of your efforts and expertise. Whenever possible, begin the education before you begin to provide the service. In the landscape industry, for example, professionals often take the property owner on an initial walk-through. At this time, they discuss what the owner would like to see done to the property, and the landscaper shares information on how those objectives will be accomplished, the number of labor hours involved, and other considerations.

> *"I wish it were that easy to design an automatic lawn sprinkler system. To ensure that your system works correctly—that water isn't backing up on itself and proper pressure is maintained—we need to look more closely at the elevation of your yard. Let me show you a couple of examples and walk you through the process. Then, if you do decide to go on on your own, you'll know what to expect."*

"But the check is in the mail."

The toughest discussions to hold with customers, and the toughest to avoid, are questions about money—especially past-due money. People don't like to talk about debt—they don't talk about it very easily or, openly, or for long.

Four guidelines will smooth the way when you have to ask the question "Where is your payment?"

1. *Don't wait to discuss issues of nonpayment.* The longer a customer delays paying you, the harder it will be to collect the debt and the more it will cost you to do so. Address delinquent payment issues early, within the first sixty to ninety days after the payment is due.

2. When discussing a debt, *separate the debt from the person.* Use phrases such as "your account shows" rather than "you owe." There are many reasons why customers may withhold payment. Never intending to pay is only one of them. It may be your customer is unhappy with some aspect of your service or product and is withholding payment as a way to get even. Or your customer may be experiencing a cash-flow problem based on seasonal issues or on payments needed from his or her customers. Separating the debt from the person will help you hold a positive conversation in which your customer may surface those issues and lead to a creative solution.

3. *Reward customers who pay on time.* Consider offering a discount to customers who pay promptly. A reward for prompt payment is often more effective than a penalty for late payment. Consider totaling up the dollar value of the "on-time discount" and referring to it in a thank-you letter to prompt-paying clients.

4. *Start with trust.* Until experience teaches you otherwise, believe your customer when he or she says, "The check is in

the mail." Even when the check is not, that statement is often code for, "The check will be in the mail *today. I'll mail it right now!"* Allow some time for the check to arrive. Sometimes checks do go astray.

Variation: "So sue me. I'm not going to pay."

Perhaps taking a truculent customer up on the offer to "sue me" will in a few cases cause the customer to pay up on the spot. More often than not, it will lead to protracted court proceedings. And if going to court eventually *does* work, it may forever injure your relationship with the customer—your ability to do business together again. So, help your company think long and hard before taking legal action.

An independent interior decorator we know began purchasing refurbished toner cartridges for her laser printer. The company she contracted with "owned" the plastic cartridge itself and asked that the cartridge be exchanged for refurbishing each time the toner ran out. Our friend was happy with the service and even served as a reference for potential customers. However, problems with her finicky printer prompted her to change to new, rather than refurbished cartridges. After waiting weeks for the supplier to pick up the cartridge, she threw the cartridge away. Months later, she received a bill for one hundred dollars to cover the cost of replacing the cartridge. She explained why she felt the bill was unfair and why she would not pay it. She expected this to prompt dialogue and some sort of adjustment—perhaps a "we'll pay half if you'll pay half" compromise. Instead, her next contact came in the form of a summons to small claims court.

Yes, the toner company did finally receive a check for one hundred dollars from our friend. But the company salesperson who called on our friend two months later to sell her toner service got an earful about how "hell would have to freeze over" before she—or anyone she knows—would ever consider doing business with the company again.

"Can't you make an exception to the rule?"

We all live and work with mountains of rules, regulations, and standard operating procedures. There are a lot of reasons for rules—some good, some not so good. Some rules have a lot more to do with the convenience of someone in inventory control or the accounting department than the convenience of customers. For example, a movie theater concession stand that counts drink cups the end of each shift in order to monitor and manage soft drink sales might have a rule warning: *"Do not give out drink cups for water."*

Other rules are designed to keep things neat, straight, and running smoothly: *"Would the person who drinks the last cup of coffee please make a new pot."*

Still others are created to ensure employee and customer safety: *"No one allowed on the construction site without a hard hat."*

Don't expect your customers to know your rules, much less understand them. That's your job; be clear and up-front about what the rules are, and know when you can and can't allow exceptions to them.

A helpful technique for getting a better handle on the rules that surround the work you do is to classify each rule as "red" or "blue." Red rules cannot be broken. They have life-or-death—or at least, employment versus unemployment—consequences. They are the "laws" that *govern* the way things are done. Blue rules, in contrast, are important *guides* for doing work. They may be bent or broken. If a rule is blue, an exception may be considered. Knowing exactly when and how to make an exception to the blue rules, like many things, is easier said than done. There are three flavors of exception; *the little favor,* the *big favor,* and the *"special" customer.*

1. *The Little Favor.* Little favors are exceptions to blue rules that are no big deal to you or the company but that can mean

a great deal to customers. They are generally easy, but we talk about them here, as part of No Easy Answers, because you do need to proceed with caution. If customers perceive your "little favor" as a normal business practice, they will expect it every time.

Customer: **"I know the drug store doesn't open 'til 8:00 A.M., but since you're here, can I drop off this film?"**

Store Employee: **"You are in luck! You've stopped by on just about the only morning I am ready enough to take your film."**

2. *The Big Favor.* At times customers want to be excused from rules that have greater impact for you, your coworkers, and the organization as a whole. When deciding whether to bend or break a blue rule, there are three issues to consider. First, will this exception cause too much delay in serving other customers? Second, will it inconvenience another department in an unacceptable way? Third, is this a request you should pass along to a supervisor?

Bank customers frequently become tangled in rules, policies, and procedures. A common confusion involves the length of time banks hold a deposited check before making those funds available for withdrawal. Customers may know that the bank reserves the right to hold the deposited check for five days, but may, in practice, rely on the fact that checks drawn on local banks are usually available in only one or two days.

"I don't understand how I got an overdraft notice on my checking account. I deposited my pay-check Monday, but when I called the bank-by-phone line, they told me I have a negative balance."

The decision to make an exception to the rules for this customer—to release the funds and reverse the overdraft charges—is generally handled by a senior service specialist and may depend on several factors. The service specialist may discover that this customer honestly misunderstood the bank's "funds available" policy. In that case, the bank may "forgive" the customer:

> *"I can understand your confusion. I'll send you a flier explaining our funds available process. The money you deposited on Monday will be available to you tomorrow. In the meantime, I will make a special exception and reverse the overdraft charges and make sure no checks are returned for insufficient funds."*

A look at the notes attached to this customer's file may suggest that this customer was trying to play the rules to his or her advantage—again. In this case, the bank may be much less flexible about the policy:

> *"I am sorry, but those moneys won't be available until tomorrow. As you know, we hold your check deposit for up to five days—until we have cleared it with the other bank. I will, however, make sure no additional overdraft charges are made between now and tomorrow."*

3. *The Special Customer.* Some customers invariably seem to act as if they are the only customer we have. Or the only one that counts. And they are—to themselves. We may, and do, talk frequently about treating all customers equally. Every customer should receive equal respect and courtesy, but it is the nature of commerce that you will bend over further for some than for others. You have to—it's good business sense. And some customers know it. Your best approach is, first, to *know what the client was promised.* Don't get angry because some clients have ultra high, "treat me special" expectations—they may have them for very good reason. Because they were told your company—and you—would deliver. Find out who the key clients are for your organization.

Second, *know how far you can go to serve key clients.* The service manager for a Detroit-based metal fabrication company told us, "Hupmobile is our number one client. They provide

75 percent of our revenue. Whatever they ask for, and I mean whatever, we will find a way to do it."

For the metal fabrication company, "do whatever it takes for our key client" can supersede just about every one of the blue rules that guide employees on the job. And that's okay. Without special customers, your job might be easier . . . but then you might not have a job!

"Snow? Big deal.
Where's my paper?"

Customers have little regard for the impossible. And there are
indeed times when it's a kick to do the "impossible" for a
customer. The old motto "The difficult we do right away, the
impossible takes a little longer" is as much a sign of pride as it
is a complaint about customer demands. Still, there *are* times
when a thing cannot and will not be done—regardless of
how much the customer demands otherwise. Snowstorms,
earthquakes, fire, flood, and riot bring out strange qualities in
customers. In times of stress, some of them become demanding
boobies and resist your every request for a little understanding:

"Three feet of snow? Big deal. Where's my paper?"

Tempting as it may be to shout, in your best Scottish
accent, "Damn it, Captain. I'm an engineer, not a magician,"
don't.

Your best bet: *Prepare for the worst.* Have a "disaster recovery" plan on file for your organization, department, or unit.
Although it is impossible to predict everything that might
interrupt or impair your ability to serve customers, you can
anticipate the types of problems that may occur and how those
problems will impact service to customers.

When the worst happens and you are face to face or phone
to phone with a customer who wants what you can't do,
realize that the customer's anger and ire may well be caused by
some underlying fear or concern. Your communication should
be designed to *put that fear—real or imagined—to rest.*

On October 31, 1990, the Minneapolis/St. Paul area received
28½ inches of snow in less than twenty-four hours. City snow
plows were still set up for leaf removal. The next day, schools
were closed and hundreds of businesses were shut down as

adults and children enjoyed a "snow day." Yet at the offices of the morning newspapers in both cities, the calls began to pour in. The same people who couldn't get their cars out of their driveways, much less navigate the unplowed residential streets, wanted to know where their newspapers were and why they hadn't been delivered.

Savvy circulation staff members recognized that callers had two major concerns. The first was their inability to accept the extent of the storm's impact. If the snow could shut down the paper—something no one could remember having happened before—what else might happen? These callers wanted to be reassured that everything would be back to normal very soon. The second concern was that they would be billed for the missed delivery day. At the Minneapolis *Star Tribune*, staff responded to both concerns:

> **"You will receive a credit on your bill for today's paper. Tomorrow's paper may arrive late in some areas, depending on plowing, but it will most definitely be a keeper, with great pictures and stories about the snow!"**

In other words, they told customers to relax; everything was under control and soon would be back to normal.

Variation: "It's not unreasonable. You just don't want to do it."

A variation on this theme happens when what the customer requests is physically possible, but you and your organization have deemed it unreasonable, not a way you wish to do business. Consider our favorite local small-job printing store, City Press. We overheard a customer ask:

> **"Why can't you bump someone else's work and do mine first? I'll pay the rush fee."**

What this customer didn't realize is that the owner bases his business on making promises to customers and keeping the promises he makes. His first priority was to keep the commitments he'd already made. His reply:

> *"I wish I could accept. What I can do is check with several of my clients to find out if they can be flexible about the deadlines for their printing jobs."*

"Dog food is dog food. Isn't it?"

Whether or not the word "sales" appears in your job title or job description, you will be asked to explain how your products and services differ from those offered by your competition. After all, many customers innately believe that "dog food is dog food" and will challenge you to explain why your dog food, or printing services, or convention space, or health care services, or automobiles are better than—or at the very least, different from—your competition's.

There is a simple rule of thumb: *Find out*. Ask around. Ask the salespeople and the manufacturing and operations specialists. Ask customers and executives. Read the marketing and sales literature. Even if you don't personally make it or hawk it, your customers have every right to expect you to be able to talk about it. Intelligently. Persuasively.

It doesn't matter if your customers are external or internal. The manager of an in-house printing unit was amazed to discover that many members of his delivery staff didn't like talking with customers. "Customers always ask us why we cost more than the quick-copy place on the corner. I don't know what to say," one explained. With the manager's encouragement, a small group got together and worked out an answer that every employee in the unit could adapt and use when customers bring up the topic of cost:

> *"If you want the cheapest copies in terms of the price per page, sometimes you do have to go to the place on the corner. But that price doesn't include the service and convenience we offer. We're right here in your building, so it takes only a few minutes for us to walk to your floor and pick up or deliver your work. We also think we have unbeatable quality. It's not just your name on the*

materials you create; it's our company name, too. And we're set up to ensure consistency between all of the materials created by all of the various parts of our organization. We can serve as designers on new brochure creation and consultants on binder design. All told, we believe we are very competitive."

Sure, it's a lengthy answer. And the employees seldom run through it in one fell swoop. Just the same, having a "rap" that explains and justifies the department's philosophy has had an ego-boosting effect on morale.

"If you don't do exactly as I say, I'm going to take my business somewhere else."

Some customers will use any means, any form of pressure, to get us to do what they want in exactly the way they demand it be done. They will even make the ultimate threat—"If you don't do exactly as I say, I'm going to take my business somewhere else." There are, of course, some customers we wish would make that threat just so we can have the pleasure of waving good-bye. But the customer who seeks to kidnap our cooperation through threats and outrageous behavior brings us to a good question: "Is there ever a time to 'lose'—as in *fire*—a customer?"

There are two issues to consider when answering that question:

1. *Is this customer relationship profitable?* In answering this question, consider not only the gross profits from sales to this customer but also the cost of serving this customer—the cost in time, stress, and, possibly, higher employee turnover. A rule of thumb: It costs fifty dollars per hour for the average hourly wage employee to argue with a customer.

2. *Does continuing this customer relationship, in this manner, fit with your organization's business values?* One manager told us, "I always tell my people they have the right to expect respect on the job. I was appalled to learn of the gross and threatening things one of our customers had been saying to some of my staff. I put an end to it, but they'd been hearing it for weeks

and not telling me. I don't want any customer to believe he can get what he wants from us through that sort of behavior."

If the answer to one or both of these questions is "no," it is time to consider seriously giving this customer a chance to become someone else's opportunity. We saw this situation played out at an executive office suite company. Standard operating procedure held that if a prime corner office was vacated, it would be rented to an established client according to a waiting list. Showing space to a prospective tenant, the office manager walked by a recently vacated corner office. With the door open, he couldn't miss the magnificent view. "This is exactly what I've been looking for," exclaimed the prospect. When the office manager explained that she couldn't rent that office to him, he became belligerent and said "Fine. If you don't rent me that corner office, I'm going to rent from your competition." The office manager stuck to her guns. With tact and grace, she restated her position:

> *"I'm really sorry you feel that way. I think we offer the best space and office support services in the area. I'm sorry you won't be part of our group."*

An interesting thing happened. Two weeks later, the prospect called the office manager and apologized for his outburst. He then asked if there were still other office vacancies he could look at. This client still rents from that company. Sometimes it takes drawing a line in the sand—saying we will do this much and no more—to earn customer respect.

Note: You may not be the person who gets to make the decision to sever a customer relationship. That call is most often made by senior management. However, those decision makers need information and assessment from *you* in order to make good decisions.

Variation: "Excuse me, but there's a fight going on in the waiting area."

Related, we think, to "do what I say, or else" situations are those times you must deal with individuals exhibiting

threatening or abusive behavior. Of course, if such behavior becomes violent, your response is clear—call 911 and building security, no ifs, ands, or buts. However, there is a wealth of inappropriate behavior that should be addressed long before the "Officer needs assistance" stage.

A two-step approach seems to work best. First, if possible, separate the inappropriately behaving person or persons from the rest of your customers. Perhaps the easiest way to do this is to "walk" the upset customer to another area of your business or to a more private meeting area. Simply maintain eye contact while moving toward the target area—most customers will follow without even realizing they are being led. Or you may choose to suggest a move. The manager of a brokerage office was startled to hear loud yelling in the lobby. She found two clients holding an impassioned argument, much to the discomfiture of the other customers and staff. She broke into their "discussion" with:

"Hello, gentlemen. We have a conference room available right over here if you'd like to continue this discussion with some privacy."

The second step is to deal with the inappropriate behavior. For the brokerage clients, the manager's interruption and calm handling of the situation was all they needed to stop yelling; they later apologized. Other times you may have to do more. Three tactics will help you deal with what we've come to call "Customers From Hell."™ First, *ignore the behavior and focus on the real issue.* This is easier said than done. However, we've learned that most of the individuals who appear to be "Customers From Hell" are actually "Customers Who've Been Through Hell"—think of their behavior as a slide show of their trip. Smile and nod and listen for the real issue, the real complaint.

Second, *surface the tension.* If their rantings and ravings feel personal, find out if they are. Ask:

"Have I done something personally to upset you? I'd like to be part of the solution."

Nine times out of ten, this question will pull customers up short, remind them that you are, in fact, a person who can assist them, and prompt them to tell you about the real problem or need.

What if their answer is, "Yes, as a matter of fact you have personally ruined my life!"? Well, that is important information to know. If a misunderstanding is at the root of their ire, now is your chance to clear it up.

If you can't solve the problem, move on to the third tactic: *Transfer this customer to a coworker or manager.* If a particular customer absolutely, positively refuses to work with you, to allow you to solve the problem or fill the need, even though you are perfectly capable of doing so, don't force the issue. Instead, graciously involve another member of your service team. Be advised: The customer your coworker sees may seem very different from the customer who was just melting your phone. When your coworker says, "Gee, that was one of the nicest people I've ever spoken with. What did you say to upset her?" remember that the reason this tactic works is that it offers the customer a chance to transform—to leave the upset, anger, and negative behavior in the past with you and to show a better side to the next service representative.

Part 4

Getting Service as Good as You Give: The Amazingly Simple Secret of the Ten-Second Connection

Cast thy bread upon the waters; for thou shalt find it
returned after many days.

Ecclesiastes 11:1

All is not gold that glitters.

Latin proverb

Civility costs nothing.

Proverb

He gets as good as he gives, and he gives a' plenty.

William Shakespeare
Hamlet

It would be logical to assume that people who give great customer service are masters of *getting* great customer service when the roles are reversed. Logical, but wrong!

We have found that customer service pros are as likely as "civilians" to end up in seat HH in row 426 on the seventy-two-hour flight to Bogota, just as prone to getting the hotel room next to the elevator and across from the ice machine, as apt as anyone to find themselves with the restaurant table next to the kitchen door, and as inclined as the next person to show up at the shop and find their cars not finished at 5:00 P.M. as promised. And they are as disposed to being handed fresh dry cleaning and finding that the trousers or skirt they were counting on for tomorrow haven't a crease or a pleat they would want to be seen dead wearing in public. At the same time, we've noticed a tendency on the part of service pros *not* to complain about bad service and poorly done work and to excuse this unlikely timidity as professional empathy: "I know what it's like to make a mistake."

But there *is* a limit. How long can you listen politely and smile benignly as Aunt Bessie tells yet another tale of successfully challenging yet another salesperson to help her find the perfect dress and, of course, wheedling the price down 30 percent? And how long can you remain unfazed by the obvious fact that your good friend Phil down the block always seems to get a little extra help with the crab grass from the lawn-care guy, and that the UPS person seems to be extra careful that rain never touch packages delivered to his house, and that the street crew never seems to build a snow fortress across the end of *his* driveway? In other words, how long *can* you go through life *not* demanding service as good as you give?

And one more thing: After studying the ways and wiles of those who consistently *get* great service—called Service Magnets for the way good service seems drawn to them—we have become convinced that the better you become at getting great service, the more expanded your capacity to give great service becomes. You can't give away what you don't own, and you can't own what you aren't willing to stand up for.

The Attitude of Being Served Well

Challenged first by the example of our colleague Chip Bell, a Service Magnet first class, who seems at times to get better service than almost anyone in the Western world, we set out to learn just what he does that we weren't doing. After several days, we expanded our search to encompass observations of other masters of the art of being served well. What we found is that Service Magnets are just like you and us except for some simple behaviors in which they regularly engage while being served and some attitudes and assumptions they tell us they carry around like credit cards—they never leave home without 'em. Let's start with the assumptions and attitudes with which the Service Magnets approach a service transaction.

Assumption 1: *You deserve good service.*
You *are* the customer. Expecting good service is your right. Expecting great service—when a tornado isn't imminent, there aren't seventy other customers waiting impatiently, and the service person isn't in obvious ill health or distemper—is

reasonable as well. Not exactly a *right,* but a reasonable expectation to hold. And when you *do* receive great service, you have an *obligation* to show your delight and thanks. The recipients of great service never confuse *deserve* with *demand.*

Assumption 2: *People enjoy giving great service.*

As you know so well, it's a lot more enjoyable telling customers "yes," solving their problems, and giving them what they want and need, than the opposite. It's as true of the people who serve you as it is of you. Gift them with the opportunity and latitude to serve you well, and they will.

Assumption 3: *Respect and goodwill are reciprocal.*

People have a tendency to return in kind the treatment they receive from others. Act the part of "The Customer From Hell" and you will receive "Nightmare on Elm Street" treatment. Turn an expressionless or bored face to the desk clerk or checkout person at the grocery store and guess what you'll get back? But show some warmth and character and . . . you get the idea. Today the phenomenon is referred to as "psychological reciprocity"; in an earlier era it was known as the "do unto others" principle.

Assumption 4: *Sometimes "no" is the right answer.*

You know that "no" is sometimes the right answer. It's fine to ask for special favors, to ask to be made an exception to policy, to wheedle a little bit—and it's okay for the service person to say, "Sorry, I just can't do that." Never make the service person any more uncomfortable than you would accept being made if the roles were reversed. At the same time, it's okay to ask for a different but related favor—one that will meet your needs in a different way—if your first request is denied. "I understand you can't upgrade us both because first class is full. Do you have a bulkhead or emergency row open, someplace with a little more leg room where we could still stretch out a little and get some work done?"

Assumption 5: *Priming the pump for the next time is important.*

Even when the service person tells you "no" or is unable to make an exception or fix the problem, thanking him or her for making an effort or just for listening is important. You *may* be back. But even if you *won't,* your civility can loosen up the service person for someone else. It's called priming the pump or casting your bread upon the waters. Consider it an important act of random kindness.

Five Steps to Better Service

The five attitudes or assumptions lead to five behavioral or action differences that separate the Service Magnets from the rest of us:

1. They prepare mentally prior to the transaction.
2. They spend time with service people at the beginning of the transaction.
3. They tell a clear story and communicate their personality to the service person.
4. They define a clear task for the service person.
5. They set a challenge for the service person.

We have translated these observations into a five-step process for getting great service that we are convinced can be learned and successfully used by anyone.

Step 1: *Prepare to be served well.* Service Magnets see themselves as the recipients of good service—literally. Several have told us that they mentally visualize being served well just before they step up to the service line. As a result, their demeanor in facing a service provider is pleasant and confident. They just *know* that they are going to be served well, and they prepare for that contingency. They then create a self-fulfilling prophesy with their words and actions. Call it the Think Method: Think good service, visualize it happening, and more often than not, it will.

Step 2: *Make the ten-second connection.* Take a deep breath and hold it for ten seconds—one thousand one, one thousand two, one thousand three, one thousand four, one thousand five, one thousand six, one thousand seven, one thousand eight, one thousand nine, one thousand ten.

Exhale. A lot longer than you thought, wasn't it? Service

Magnets use those ten seconds to make a connection with the service person, *as a person*. Service Magnets go out of their way to let service people know that they are seen as people doing important, worthwhile jobs and are not faceless functionaries or meaningless menials. Simultaneously, Service Magnets use some of those ten seconds to begin the process of establishing *themselves* as unique in the service provider's eyes. The goal is clearly to be seen as "unique" or "special" in some positive sense and not categorized as "the gall bladder in room 406" or "the passenger in seat 17C."

Go out for dinner with a Service Magnet, and you are very likely to hear patter something like: "Well, good evening to you as well. Edward, I've really been looking forward to this evening in your wonderful restaurant, and I know you're going to make it a memorable experience for me and my friends."

Or simply: "Edward, it's been a long week, and I'm looking forward to putting myself in your capable hands."

That same Service Magnet, checking into a hotel might sound like this:

Customer:	**How are you this evening, Kathy? Are you having a *great* day?**
Front-Desk Clerk:	**I'm fine. What can I do for you?**
Customer:	**Well, I've got a reservation, and I just know you are going to find a super room for me. Am I right?**
Front-Desk Clerk:	**Oh, I believe I can find one you'll like. (Big smile)**

That doesn't seem too hard, does it? But beware: Making off-task small talk and forcing a little eye contact with a service person who has spent the day talking to uninteresting people and practicing the fine art of service robotics can wilt the firmest of intentions. The key is to use whatever time it takes to make personal contact. Remember, even though you are going to spend at *most* ten seconds, it can seem an eternity when you aren't immediately receiving the attention you antic-ipated. A critical point: Pausing to wait for the service person to look up and give you his or her full attention after you've said "Hello" is often all it takes to break through the service person's mask of indifference and find the human being. But you must wait for the connection to be made, and that is very hard for most people to do.

Step 3: *Reveal a little of your personality.* As soon as the connection is established, Service Magnets reveal a little bit of their personalities, and a little of their "story" to the service rep.

"Edward, I started thinking about having dinner here this evening when I stepped on the plane home at 6 A.M. this morning."

"Jane, I can't tell you how long today has been. So I hope you have a nice quiet comfortable room available for me."

"George, I hope that dry cleaning is ready and everything is all right. If it's not, I may just have to go to work naked tomorrow!"

The sharing of personality and personal story frequently begins with the greeting in Step 1. All it takes is for that greeting to be a little out of the ordinary: "Hey, are we having

fun yet?" or "How ya'll doing tonight?" or simply "This is just a great evening, isn't it?" are greetings far enough out of the ordinary to attract the service person's attention and signal that you as a customer may be a little out of the ordinary as well. The playfulness or uniqueness or warmth of the greeting conveys "I'm interested in who you are, not just what I want from you." A Service Magnet we studied who begins every transaction with a booming Texas "Howdy! How ya'll doing?" sets an immediate ten-gallon image that invariably brings a smile to the lips of service people in the Northeast.

The philosopher Rollo May wrote, "There is a natural energy between people. When one person reaches out with passion, it is generally met with an answering passion." This passion or charisma engages the service provider as a person. Service Magnets unconsciously use this energy to rise above the crowd and set the scene for the service transaction. In a sense, Service Magnets portray themselves and the service provider as players in a story—one that is certain to have a positive ending, a story they are carefully unfolding for the service person's delight. A caution: You are not trying to make a friend for life. You are trying to brighten your own day and receive great service. That simply begins by brightening someone else's day a little bit first.

Step 4: *State your request.* Having set the stage and piqued the service provider's interest, Service Magnets now spin out their requests in the form of a short story.

"This is a really special night. Let me tell you about the kind of table I would feel fortunate to get."

"How am I this evening? To tell you the truth, it's been a long, long week and I've been looking forward to celebrating the end of it since about noon yesterday. Can you help me do just that?"

By creating a vision of the end, without dictating the "do this, do that" steps required to achieve it, Service Magnets enfold the service provider in their goal. Within the story there often is a challenge for the service provider. The skills of the service provider are directly engaged with statements such as: "What do you think?", "What would you do?", or even "This might be something you aren't able to do, but if you can, I'd really like. . . . "

One of the Service Magnets we trailed has a knack for always getting the best meal a restaurant has to offer. He doesn't even open the menu. When the waiter or waitress is ready to take his order, he smiles broadly and says: "Let me describe the kind of dinner I really enjoy—something light, unique, spicy is okay. I would like an appetizer, salad, and entree. And surprise me!" Almost invariably the waiter or waitress will bring a sampler tray from the kitchen or add a special dessert to the end of the meal.

Service Magnets bypass any "you can't tell me how to do my job" resistance on the part of the service provider, and their openness encourages achievement-oriented service providers—those who like to strut their stuff, but only for the appreciative—to go beyond the call of duty to demonstrate their skill.

Step 5: *Closing the loop.* Service Magnets not only engage service people in their wants and needs; they seek ways to reciprocate, be it through tipping, bragging to the employee's supervisor, or praising the service person loudly within earshot of other customers. They never take the service providers for granted and go out of their way to express gratitude. Sometimes, even when their expectations have not exactly been met.

Another of our colleagues, Dr. Thomas Connellan, is well remembered by people at a certain airline check-in desk in the Toronto airport. The story beings with his *thanking* them for telling him exactly what he did not want to hear:

Dr. Tom: I've been traveling for a week and I'm looking forward to getting home. What are my *real* chances for making the earlier flight?

Gate Agent: Not much—zero, really.

Dr. Tom: Well, I'm not very happy about that, but I want to thank you for telling me. Now, I know what to do with my time until the next flight.

The next time Tom came through the Toronto airport, the gate agent—whom Tom remembered as "being shocked" when Tom thanked him for his honesty—came out from behind the counter and walked him on board and told the crew to give "his friend" extra-special treatment.

Service Magnets more often than not write letters to the front-line people who serve them well, their supervisors and managers, and the CEOs of their companies. And they tell others about their great service experiences, encouraging their colleagues to tell the service person, "I've heard that you are absolutely the best!"

Easy To Talk About

In the end, we found that getting great service is as much about *giving* as it is about *receiving*. Oh, sure, it's probably true that the rich and famous need not play by these rules. But for the rest of us, getting great service, becoming a Service Magnet, is a reciprocal process—what we give in time, attention, and a little human kindness comes back in helpfulness, attention, and courtesy. And the feeling of two jobs well done.

Part 5

Customers Say the Darnedest Things

Humor is a prelude to faith, and laughter is the
beginning of prayer.

Reinhold Niebuhr

No mind is thoroughly well organized, that is deficient in
a sense of humor.

Samuel Taylor Coleridge

If you don't genuinely like your customers, they will
genuinely dislike you.

Anonymous

We know, as do you, that it is important to respect, speak, and think well of your customers and clients. Nothing sours relations with a customer faster than disdain and lack of respect.

At the same time, it is also true that customers can inadvertently—and sometimes with tongue planted firmly in cheek—say odd, interesting, and very funny things. Remembering, recounting, sharing, and enjoying such incidents doesn't show disrespect—just a fine sense of fun, and appreciation for the accidental, the serendipitous, the misspoken, and the willfully witty. Since publication of our book *Delivering Knock Your Socks Off Service*, we have invited customer service reps we've met around the world to share with us their most memorable moments of customer craziness—the strange, unusual, funny, and perplexing comments, questions, complaints, and pronouncements they have heard from their customers. Along the way we've learned two things: first, many customers do have a great sense of humor, even about gaffes, foul-ups, and service breakdowns; second, as Shakespeare put it so long ago:

> What a piece of work is Man!
> How noble in reason!
> How infinite in Faculty!

And how truly enjoyable and fun to serve well, especially when you remember that every one of us is somebody else's customer—and as likely to err, frustrate, and misspeak as are *our* customers.

Presented on the following pages for your casual entertainment and enlightenment are seventy-five of the most unusual, interesting, amusing, pithy things customer service people report hearing from *their* customers.* May they brighten your day just a little bit and serve to remind you why you get up in the morning, brush your teeth, comb your hair, rush off to the office or store, take that first phone call, look that first customer in the eye, put a smile in your voice, and ask, "Good morning. How may I help you?"

Overcome by Technology—High and Low

Computers take the measure of us all from time to time. Sometimes it's something as seemingly simple as finding the on/off switch that sends the new computer user running for the customer service help line.

Customer: I just bought one of your new laptop computers and I'm having a problem.
CSR: What's the problem?
Customer: I unpacked it, plugged it in, opened it up, and have been waiting for twenty minutes.
CSR: Exactly what happened when you pressed the power switch?
Customer: What power switch?

The *Wall Street Journal*
March 1, 1994

CSR: You'll have to make up a new password.
Customer: Okay. [Long pause]

*We thank the editors and staff of Lakewood Publications' newsletter for helping us collect and compile many of these stories through our "Customers Say the Darnedest Things" contests. Anecdote contributors are acknowledged wherever possible, and as thoroughly as we have space and information to do so.

CSR: **Sir? What's happening?**
Customer: **I made up a new password and nothing happened. Oh! Was I supposed to key it in?**

Rich Simek, Grumman Data Systems
Long Island, N.Y.

Sometimes the frustration comes from the effort of translating tech-manual English into real English.

I just paid three thousand dollars for this thing and I'm not going to read any book. You're going to tell me how to use it!

The *Wall Street Journal*
March 1, 1994

Sometimes it's simply the need to register their frustrations that sends users to the phones.

If I log on correctly, enter data correctly, transmit claims successfully, and complete this all in record-breaking time, will you hire me as a consultant?

Judy Milo, ProMed Systems
New Haven, Conn.

Customer: **I've pushed and pushed on the foot pedal and I can't get this computer started.**
CSR: **Foot pedal?**
Customer: **Yea, this white thing with the little ball on the bottom and the clicker at the top.**

Dell Computer Corp.
The *Wall Street Journal*, March 1, 1994

What database do I search to get information on the calcification of wombats' toes?

Dayle Smidt, Dialog Information Systems
Palo Alto, Calif.

Library Patron: **Do you have computers here?**
Librarian: **Yes.**
Patron: **And you keep a record of the books on it?**

Librarian:	Yes.
Patron:	Oh, good. Could you ask it which books I've read? I forget and I don't want to read any of 'em over again.

Terrie Miller, Anoka County Library
Anoka, Minn.

Customer:	Could you please look up my account?
CSR:	Yes, sir. I'll need your social security number or your policy number.
Customer:	I don't know those. Can't you just go by my name?
CSR:	Yes, sir. May I have your name?
Customer:	John Smith.

Liz Davis, Aetna Life Insurance & Annuity Co.
Hartford, Conn.

And sometimes they simply throw in the towel.

Could you quit your job, move to LA, and go to work for me? I'll give you fifty thousand dollars to start, and a million-dollar budget to set me up a library.

Dayle Smidt, Dialog Information Systems
Palo Alto, Calif.

Computers, as we said earlier, aren't the only source of confusion in our lives. Lesser technological wonders take our measure from time to time as well.

Could you please tell me which speed dial button you are on my telephone?

Sherri Holdeman, First of America Services
Kalamazoo, Mich.

I know my payment is due today. Can I just fax you my check?

Joyce Applegate
Cedar Falls, Iowa

I'm using one of your cake mixes. I was wondering if it would be okay to boil an egg on top of the stove while the oven is running?

General Mills, Inc.
Minneapolis, Minn.

I took my Christmas tree down last night and now my cable box doesn't seem to be working. Do I need a repair person?

Sharon Bokstein, Cablenet Ltd.
Burlington, Ontario

This car battery charger—can I just plug it into my cigarette lighter, then connect it to my battery to recharge it?

A. L. Thrasher, Thrasher's Hardware
Des Moines, Iowa

CSR: **We can fax those papers if you'd like.**
Customer: **Oh, we don't have a fax. But we do have a Xerox machine—will that work?**

Colleen Bonneville, Norwest Funding
Minneapolis, Minn.

Is There a Doctor in the House—Or Somebody?

Navigating the modern health-care delivery system and the web of insurance providers that pay for it confuses the most sophisticated among us. Our queries and comments to customer service reps in both those businesses reveal just how flummoxed we can be by the whole experience. As one exasperated customer was overheard to say as he filled out the third of four forms at a hospital admissions desk, "If you aren't sick when you get here, you will be before you leave."

Isn't "neurology" and "urology" the same except for the spelling?

Ava Parker-Winford, Group Health Cooperative
Seattle, Wash.

Sometimes the crazy quilt of PPOs, HMOs, health insurance companies, self-insured plans, Medicaid and Medicare, co-pays and permissions can cause customers to see the system as an unfathomable blur.

Caller:	**I had a whole bunch of tests done yesterday by my doctor.**
Insurance CSR:	**Yes?**
Caller:	**I called my doctor but he's not in.**
Insurance CSR:	**Yes?**
Caller:	**Well, can't *you* tell me what's wrong with me?**

Mike Kata, CIGNA Health Care
Bristol, Conn.

A tree in my yard fell on my head. Is my medical treatment covered under my homeowner's policy?

Sarane Heggen, PruPac
Hinsdale, Ill.

And lest we've given the impression that it's just we civilians who are confused by health care and associated services, consider this urgent query from a worried insurance agent:

The medical requirements for my client are for a urine specimen and a blood sample. So how do I get the blood?

Beverly Rossell, Meredian Life Insurance Co.
Indianapolis, Ind

Dollars and Nonsense

Maybe it's the arithmetic. Certainly it's all the "gee-whiz" news stories about the marriage of high tech and financial

management and what the really smart investor would be doing today that raise our expectations—and confusion level. Whatever the origin, we are indeed muddled by matters financial.

Customer:	Why did you bounce my check? It says void if written for less than $100. I wrote it for more than that!
CSR:	How much did you write it for?
Customer:	$19,000.
CSR:	I'm sorry, but you only have $2,000 in your account.
Customer:	I guess I'll have to take the car back.

Kirstin Tompkins, Oppenheimer Funds
Denver, Colo.

My account can't be overdrawn! I still have checks in my check book!

Sharon Bayless, Citizens Banking Company
Wintersville, Ohio

Does it cost more to use blue or black ink when writing a check?

Lisa Cannovo, Magna Bank
St. Louis, Mo.

Customer:	If a check I wrote to a furniture store was lost in the mail and never cleared my account, could you locate who has the check?
CSR:	Gee, I don't think so. . . .
Customer:	You mean to tell me you can't put a tracer on the check, even if I gave you the exact location of the mailbox and the time I mailed it?

Tracy Burton, Point Mugu Federal Credit Union
Point Mugu, Calif.

Customer:	You keep sending me these notices about being overdrawn on my account.
CSR:	Yes, sir, that's correct.
Customer:	But I have one of those special revolving accounts.
CSR:	Sir?

Customer: Yeah. I write checks all month, then at the end,
you tell me what I owe, right?

Carol Peloso, The Citizens Banking Co.
Alliance, Ohio

**If I pay off my mortgage loan, will that cause a
reduction in the principal balance?**

Ann Hines, Republic Mortgage Insurance Co.
Worthington, Ohio

**Hi, I'm trying to balance my checkbook. Can
you tell me which checks I wrote that haven't
cleared yet?**

Angela Galligan, Evan-Moor
Monterey, Calif.

**If I change when I receive my statements from
monthly to quarterly, then I'll earn more money
on my account, right?**

Chelyn Hawkins, Oppenheimer Shareholder Services
Denver, Colo.

Customer: What does account closed actually mean?
CSR: You are overdrawn, and we won't honor any
more checks.
Customer: Why are you doing that?
CSR: You never deposited any money in your account.
Customer: What? Nobody ever told me I had to deposit
money to write checks!

Kim Potter, Magna Bank
St. Louis, Mo.

But not all the confusions of modern life involve technology, money, and health care. Sometimes even the long ago and far away can bewilder us. Take these snippets collected and contributed by Ray Farber, who works in the gift shop of New York's Metropolitan Museum of Art.

Customer: [*After examining a collection of jewelry repro-
ductions from the museum's Egyptian galleries*]
Young man, what is the name of King Tut's jewelry
designer?

Member:	I understand the nineteenth-century European painting and sculpture galleries will be reopening this week.
CSR:	Yes, sir, that is correct.
Member:	Can you tell me will the artists be attending?

Close Encounters of the Strangest Kind

There are days when every other customer seems to have slept under the bed *and* gotten up on the wrong side as well. And then there are those days when every third customer is on vacation from the Twilight Zone. By quitting time you feel just a little bit like calling out, "Beam me up, Scotty. I've been here way too long!"

Customer:	Is this the cable company?
CSR:	Yes, sir.
Customer:	You need to fix my converter box.
CSR:	What seems to be the problem.
Customer:	Every night about 3:00 A.M. it starts playing wine cooler theme songs.

David Levenson, New Channels Corp.
E. Syracuse, N.Y.

Customer:	I saw your ad for floating memory calculators, and I have a question.
CSR:	Yes, ma'am. What can I help you with?
Customer:	Is that memory made from the brains of unborn babies?
CSR:	Certainly not!
Customer:	Good. Let me ask you another question. That degausser you advertise—will it eliminate the noise I hear in my head when I walk by the police department and the fire station? I think they bugged my head when I wasn't looking.

Susan Davis, Tandy/Radio Shack
Ft. Worth, Tex.

Customer:	I received this notice that you are closing my account.

Manager: Yes, ma'am. I'm sorry, but we have to do that.

Customer: Well, if you close my account, none of the little animals and birdies will come into the bank anymore, and all your plants will die. I promise.

Ray Pratt, Busey Bank
Champaign, Ill.

Resident: Is this City Hall?

CSR: Yes, it is. How may I help you?

Resident: Some people from McDonnell Douglas are tunneling under this part of town.

CSR: Why are they doing that?

Resident: They have powerful airplane machinery down there that they use to make cocaine pellets, and they sell drugs and commit murders down there and there are dead bodies in the tunnels.

CSR: Have you informed the police?

Resident: Oh, yes. But they hid the tunnels, and then they robbed my house and made tire tracks on the lawn to warn me.

CSR: Are you by any chance the lady who wears tin foil on her feet to ward off gamma rays?

Resident: Why, yes. How did you know?

Anonymous
Lakewood, Calif.

[Letter received at Super 8 Motels corporate headquarters]

To whom it may concern:
We stayed in one of your motels last week. In the middle of the night my wife woke up and saw a ghost in the room. This is to inform you that we will not stay in that motel again until you can assure us it has been exorcised of all spirits.

Kristie Scherbendre, Super 8 Motels
Aberdeen, S.D.

Newspapers seem to receive a disproportionate number of calls from denizens of "The Zone," most in search of perfect service.

Can you have my carrier get down and ring my

door bell when she delivers my paper? My alarm clock doesn't work so well.

Jesse Luna, Arizona Republic Newspapers
Phoenix, Ariz.

Caller:	**I want to start a subscription.**
CSR:	**Great, what's your address?**
Caller:	**I'm not sure. I just live here in the winters.**
CSR:	**I'm afraid I need an address.**
Caller:	**Come on. I'm in Apache Junction, right across from the Circle K store. You know where that is.**

Iris Oligschlaeger, Phoenix Newspapers Inc.
Phoenix, Ariz.

When customer service specialist Brenda Beaven's photo appeared in the paper, along with the statement that she stood ready to help customers of the paper, a subscriber called and asked what days Brenda had available, explaining:

I can get in and out of bed, but could use assistance with a few things around the house.

Tammy Janz, The *Frankfort Times*
Frankfort, Ind.

Customer:	**I'm calling to follow up on a complaint letter I wrote about one of your motel managers.**
CSR:	**Yes, sir, I have it here.**
Customer:	**I was never informed of the no-pets policy when I made the reservation. Then I was asked to leave. Outrageous!**
CSR:	**If you didn't know there was a no-pet policy, why were you pushing your dog through the bathroom window when the manager walked in?**

Lori Nehlich, Super 8 Motels
Aberdeen, S.D.

Come the end of one of those Twilight Zone days, it's tempting to agree with a customer of Mike Reams of Foster & Galagher, Inc., of Peoria, Illinois, who, at the end of a long call, necessitated by a very confused order she had mailed the company, sighed and suggested:

Customer: **Let's blame it all on the stars.**
Mike: **On the stars?**
Customer: **Yes. Mercury is in the retrograde and nothing has gone right all week.**

Mike Reams, Foster & Gallagher, Inc.
Peoria, Ill.

Thank You For Sharing That . . . I Think

Every customer service person has had the urge to blurt out, "Please don't tell me any more. I already know more than I want to." That impulse is followed closely by the dreaded urge to add, "I know I'm going to regret this, but why do you ask?"

Customer: **I'm going to Atlanta.**
CSR: **Yes, sir.**
Customer: **Do I, like, need a passport for Georgia?**

Kim Loftin, NS Travel
New Bern, N.C.

Can you hold the line for a minute? My dog is eating my money, and my child is climbing out the window.

Mike Reams, Foster & Gallagher, Inc.
Peoria, Ill.

About this application. I'm in the middle of a sex change operation. So which name do I put on the account, his or hers?

Debbie Pierce, Central Illinois Lighting Company
Peoria, Ill.

If I get intoxicated by a legal alcoholic beverage and injured due to a fall, will CIGNA cover the medical expenses?

Edward Geiger, CIGNA Health Care
Bristol, Conn.

So let's say that I went hunting in the mountains and say I rented a mule, and say there was an accident, and say the mule was accidentally shot. Would you pay for the mule under my homeowners policy?

Connie Willcox, National General Insurance Co.
St. Louis, Mo.

If I fertilize my lawn this morning, will I be able to go shopping this afternoon?

Dru Gibson, The Scotts Co.
Marysville, Ohio

What fabric would be most useful for resisting urine, feces, throw-up, and blood?

Freddye Zipman, Maharam
Hauppauge, N.Y.

Caller: **Is this the storage place?**
CSR: **Yes, it is.**
Caller: **Can I store my parents there?**

Robert McCrossin, Shugard Storage Centers
St. Louis, Mo.

Customer: **I need this film developed.**
CSR: **Ma'am, I don't believe this film has been exposed.**
Customer: **Oh, my God! Can you do something? Like make magic and make a week of vacation pictures appear on the film?**

Sheri Lazzaro, Konica Quality Photo
Mt. Laurel, N.J.

Teller: How are you?
Customer: Slow and easy, dear. Slow and easy!

Karen Woody, Citizens Banking Company
East Palestine, Ohio

Oh, Never Mind

Sometimes customers and customer service people alike are sure that they are absolutely positively right—until the dawn comes. Then, well, "Never mind."

Hello. I just called in and spoke with Dave. And I told him the roses and lilacs I bought from you were dead and I wasn't going to pay for them. Well, when I got off the phone my husband told me they were just on the other side of the house. So, never mind.

Wendy Braun, Foster & Galagher, Inc.
Peoria, Ill.

Customer: Do you remember when I called and told you that the meter reader stole the chicken that was defrosting on my counter?
CSR: Yes.
Customer: And you remember that you sent a supervisor out to find the meter reader and get my chicken back?
CSR: Yes.
Customer: Well, my husband didn't want chicken for dinner, and he put it back in the freezer. So, never mind.

Ann Purvee, Rochester Gas & Electric
Rochester, N.Y.

Drive-up teller: *[to customer in pick-up truck with crutches in the passenger seat]* "What happened to your leg?"
Customer: Huh?
Teller (loudly):   Your leg. What happened to your leg?

Customer:	**Nothin'. Don't have one.**

Donna Mader, The Citizens Banking Company
Richmond, Ohio

Caller:	**I'd like to place an order.**
CSR:	**Okay, what would you like?**
Caller:	**I don't know.**
CSR:	**Would you like wall covering, upholstery, or drapery?**
Caller:	**I don't know.**
CSR:	**I need to have some idea of what you'd like if I'm to help you.**
Caller:	**Oh. . . . Never mind.**

Freddye Zipman, Maharam
Hauppauge, N.Y.

Patron:	**How dare you charge full price for these books? They're all used. I can buy brand-new ones any place in town.**
Librarian:	**But ma'am, we don't sell them, we loan them out. Free.**
Patron:	**Oh. Never mind.**

Kathy B., Anoka County Library
Anoka, Minn.

Caller:	**I'm having trouble finding the person who surveyed my lot.**
CSR:	**Let me check with someone. Can you hold? [A minute later]**
CSR:	**I asked, and I'm told he died several years ago.**
Caller:	**That's odd. I just talked with him this morning. I just haven't been able to reach him since.**

Margaret Mechlenberg, David Laird Associates
Erie, Pa.

The Answer Is Blowing in the Wind

Sometimes, customers seem to expect customer service people to be awfully knowledgeable—psychic, even. And there is a great temptation to blurt, "One moment while I consult my crystal ball for that answer."

CSR: I'm sorry, sir, she's on another call. May I take
              a message?
Caller: That depends. How long will she be?

Buff Adams, Holiday Systems
New York, N.Y.

**I was thinking about doing some investing. What
day will you be making the Strategic Income
Fund go back up?**

Stephanie Hastings, Oppenheimer Funds
Denver, Colo.

Customer: I want to go to see my daughter.
CSR: Yes, sir.
Customer: I want to get the cheapest ticket I can.
CSR: Perfectly understandable, sir.
Customer: So when will the next airline fare war be?

Tammy Job, Cook Travel
Billings, Mont.

Caller: We received this clear plastic bag with another
              laboratory's name on it. There is a pink bottle in
              the bag, and there's no label on the bottle. Well,
              we know that they get some of their bottles from
              you.
CSR: Yes.
Caller: So can you tell us what's in the bottle?

Gail Delaney, American Medical Laboratories
Chantilly, Va.

**I want to know if my son is enrolling for classes
and asking me to finance the registration fees
just so he can continue fooling around, or is he
serious about preparing for a career and getting
an education.**

Josette Guajardo, Southwestern College
Chula Vista, Calif.

Caller: Is this the help desk?
CSR: Yes.
Caller: We just received a package in the mail.
CSR: Yes.

Caller: **Well, can you tell us where it came from?**

Sheri Holdman, First of America Services
Kalamazoo, Mich.

Words Escape Us . . . Frequently

Sometimes, customers find themselves at a loss for words. Sometimes they don't, and we wish they had. And sometimes the words they do find are, well, a little strange.

Customer: **Do you carry replacement parts for toilets?**
CSR: **Yes, we do. What can I get for you?**
Customer: **I need a thing-a-ma-jig that connects to the wat-cha-ma-call-it.**

Taylor Walker, Sheridan Lumber
Hollywood, Fla.

Doesn't stainless steel come in some other color?

Dick Saylor, Phoenix of Texas
Houston, Tex.

Do you have lumber that is killed and dried?

David Perrin, Brooks Lumber
Greensboro, N.C.

Caller: **I'm having a perception problem with my TV.**
CSR: **Yes?**
Caller: **Yeah. It's all fuzzy.**

Tim Krist, Video Cable TV
Manitoba, Canada

Customer: **I'd like to move some funds from CDs into one of the fund options.**
CSR: **Certainly. Which fund would you like to move the money into?**
Customer: **The Screwball Fund.**
CSR: **Do you mean the Scudder Fund?**
Customer: **Screwball, scoodle, scrodel, whatever. The one that's doing well.**

Jackie Griggs, Aetna Life and Annuity Co.
Hartford, Conn.

CSR: Could I speak with Mr. Jones?
Spouse: He's at court.
CSR: Oh, he's a lawyer.
Spouse: No. He's a tennis player.

Ellen Bauer, CUNA Mutual Insurance Company
Waverly, Iowa

Clerk: Let's see, you need that glass cut sixteen inches
             wide by twelve inches in length, right?
Customer: Certainly not! I said twelve inches wide and six-
             teen inches in length.
Clerk: Sorry. Will there be anything else?
Customer: I also need a metric croissant wrench.

A. L. Thrasher, Thrasher Hardware
Des Moines, Iowa

**The baking instructions on the package say
"add one cup plus two tablespoons." What sort
of a spice is plus?**

General Mills, Inc.
Minneapolis, Minn.

**Can you provide me with certificates of sanity
so I can order your roses and take them with me
to Europe?**

Carla Down, Foster & Gallagher
Peoria, Ill.

[Conversation overheard by Terry, who works at the Metropolitan Museum of Art in Columbus, Ohio]

Child: What's that?
Mother: It's a sphinx.
Child: Where did it come from?
Mother: Las Vegas.

Subscriber: Is this the paper?
CSR: Yes, may I help you?
Subscriber: I want to know what you're going to do about re-
             funds?
CSR: Refunds?
Subscriber: You bet. The front page of your paper says "Final

**Edition" and I'm paid up through the last of the
month.**

Jim Batt, Phoenix Newspapers, Inc.
Phoenix, Ariz.

And finally, there are some things customers say that are
eternal, universal, and transcendent. They give us solace that,
amidst all the change around us, some things endure forever.
This, reported by Ann Wilson, of the Central Illinois Lighting
Company, Peoria, Illinois, makes the point with gold stars.

Customer: **My dog ate my disconnect notice.**
Ms. Wilson: **Is there any reason why you didn't call us when
your dog ate the notice?**
Customer: **He ate the phone book, too!**

Appendix: Recommended Resources

As we mentioned in the introduction, enhancing your customer service knowledge is a never-ending process. With that in mind, we offer the following short listing of books, newsletters, magazines, and associations.

Books

Albrecht, Karl. *At America's Service*. Homewood, Ill.: Business One Irwin, 1988.

Albrecht, Karl, and Ron Zemke. *Service America! Doing Business in the New Economy*. Homewood, Ill.: Business One Irwin, 1985.

Anderson, Kristin. *Great Customer Service on the Telephone*. New York: AMACOM Books, 1992.

Anderson, Kristin, and Ron Zemke. *Delivering Knock Your Socks Off Service*. New York: AMACOM Books, 1991.

Bell, Chip R. *Customers as Partners: Building Relationships that Last*. San Francisco: Berrett Koehler, 1994.

Bell, Chip R., and Ron Zemke. *Managing Knock Your Socks Off Service*. New York: AMACOM Books, 1992.

Berry, Leonard L. *On Great Service: A Framework for Action*. New York: Free Press, 1995.

Connellan, Thomas K., and Ron Zemke. *Sustaining Knock Your Socks Off Service*. New York: AMACOM Books, 1993.

Lash, Linda. *The Complete Guide to Customer Service*. New York: John Wiley & Sons, 1989.

Martin, William B. *Quality Customer Service*. Los Altos, Calif.: Crisp Publications, 1989.

Morgan, Rebecca L. *Calming Upset Customers*. Los Altos, Calif.: Crisp Publications, 1989.

Schaaf, Dick, and Ron Zemke. *Taking Care of Business: 101 Ways to Keep Customers Coming Back (Without Whining, Groveling or Giving Away the Store)*. Minneapolis, Minn.: Lakewood Publications, 1991.

Zemke, Ron. *The Service Edge: 101 Companies that Profit from Customer Care*. New York: New American Library, 1989.

Newsletters

The Lakewood Report, Lakewood Publications, 50 S. 9th Street, Minneapolis, MN 55402.

On Achieving Excellence, TPG Communications, 555 Hamilton Avenue, Palo Alto, CA 94301.

Customers First, Dartnell Publications, 4660 N. Ravenwood Avenue, Chicago, IL 60640.

Magazines

AFSM International: The Professional Journal
1342 Colonial Blvd., Suite 25
Ft. Myers, FL 33907

Call Center Magazine
1265 Industrial Highway
Southampton, PA 18966

Executive Excellence Magazine
Executive Excellence Publishing
3507 North University, Suite 100
Provo, UT 84606

Journal of Services Marketing
MCB University Press Limited
P.O. Box 10812
Birmingham, AL 35201–0812

Quality Digest
1350 Vista Way
P.O. Box 882
Red Bluff, CA 96080

Quality Progress
American Society for Quality Control
611 E. Wisconsin Avenue
P.O. Box 3005
Milwaukee, WI 53201–3005

Associations

Association of Field Service Managers International (AFSMI)
1342 Colonial Boulevard, Suite 25
Ft. Myers, FL 33907

International Customer Service Association (ICSA)
401 North Michigan
Chicago, IL 60611

Society of Consumer Affairs Professionals in Business
(SOCAP)
801 N. Fairfax Street, 4th Floor
Alexandria, VA 22314

International Service Quality Association (ISQA)
c/o Business Research Institute
St. John's University
Grand Central and Utopia Parkway
Jamaica, NY 11439

About the Authors

Kristin Anderson is an internationally recognized workshop leader and keynote speaker. As a principal with Performance Research Associates (PRA), Kristin specializes in customer service seminars, focus group facilitation, and survey research. Her writing has appeared in numerous publications, including *HR Magazine*, *Boardroom Reports*, and *Training* magazine. Kristin is the coauthor of *Delivering Knock Your Socks Off Service* (AMACOM) and author of *Great Customer Service on the Telephone* (AMACOM).

Ron Zemke is a management consultant, journalist, and behavioral scientist who has become one of the best-known and most widely quoted authorities on the United States's continuing service revolution. As senior editor of *Training* magazine and contributing editor of *The Lakewood Report* newsletter, he has covered the emergence and development of the global service economy. Ron has authored or coauthored twelve books, including the *Knock Your Socks Off Service* series (AMACOM) and *Service America! Doing Business in the New Economy*. He formed Performance Research Associates in 1972.

Performance Research Associates is one of North America's premier consulting firms in the related areas of service quality, customer retention, and continuous performance improvement. With offices in Minneapolis, Dallas, and Ann Arbor, the firm provides research, training, and consulting services to client organizations throughout North America and Europe.

Both Kristin and Ron, as well as other members of the PRA team, are frequent speakers at company, management, sales, and association meetings. Their presentations give practical how-tos for improving the bottom line by creating lifetime customers.